A Voice in the Wilderness

—— AN AUTOBIOGRAPHY ——

Also by Phil Drabble

BADGERS AT MY WINDOW

MY BELOVED WILDERNESS

DESIGN FOR A WILDERNESS

MY WILDERNESS IN BLOOM

PLEASING PETS

OF PEDIGREE UNKNOWN

A WEASEL IN MY MEATSAFE

ONE MAN AND HIS DOG

NO BADGERS IN MY WOOD

IT'S A DOG'S LIFE

WHAT PRICE THE COUNTRYSIDE?

Collections of articles

PHIL DRABBLE'S COUNTRY SCENE

COUNTRY SEASONS

COUNTRY WISE

COUNTRY MATTERS

COUNTRY MOODS

A VOICE IN THE WILDERNESS

—————AN AUTOBIOGRAPHY—————

Phil Drabble

ILLUSTRATED BY

Gordon Beningfield

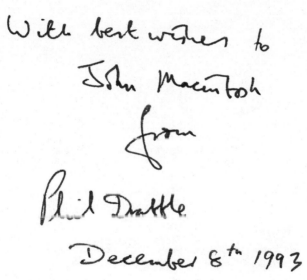

*With best wishes to
John Macintosh
from

Phil Drabble

December 8th 1993*

PELHAM BOOKS

PELHAM BOOKS

Published by the Penguin Group
Penguin Books Ltd, 27 Wrights Lane, London W8 5TZ, England
Penguin Books USA Inc., 375 Hudson Street, New York, NY 10014, USA
Penguin Books Australia Ltd, Ringwood, Victoria, Australia
Penguin Books Canada Ltd, 10 Alcorn Avenue, Suite 300, Toronto, Ontario, Canada M4V 3B2
Penguin Books (NZ) Ltd, 182–190 Wairau Road, Auckland 10, New Zealand

Penguin Books Ltd, Registered Offices: Harmondsworth, Middlesex, England

First Published 1991
3 5 7 9 10 8 6 4

Text Copyright © Phil Drabble 1991
Illustrations Copyright © Gordon Beningfield 1991

A CIP catalogue record for this book is available from the British Library
ISBN 0 7207 1908 9

Printed in England by Butler & Tanner, Frome, Somerset
Typeset in 11/13 Photina

CONTENTS

ACKNOWLEDGEMENTS

I have devoted the best part of my life to the creation of a wildlife reserve which I hope will be the first link in a national chain of similar sanctuaries which will leave the countryside better than we found it. So it came as a devastating shock when speculative developers in the mushrooming leisure industry nearly got planning consent for a development which would have ruined it.

My faith in the future was restored by the spontaneous intervention of five distinguished and impartial politicians, from Norman Tebbit, on the Right, to David Clark, Opposition Spokesman for Rural Affairs, who were prepared to cross the line of party politics to rescue a threatened sensitive environment.

I also offer my thanks to John Fletcher, the Forestry Commission Conservator, who sanctioned a pioneering exercise in creative conservation to help my own experimental wildlife management.

My admiration for his courage in putting his career and reputation on the line to safeguard our rural heritage for future generations is matched by my respect for Sir William Wilkinson, who castigated three cabinet ministers, by name, for emasculating the Nature Conservancy Council, of which he was chairman. Men with such guts should surely be protected by the Wildlife and Countryside Act which was passed to conserve specimens of rare and endangered species!

Patrick Cormack FSA, MP has been a tower of strength throughout my efforts and my friend Gordon Beningfield has not only illustrated this book and written the foreword but consented to serve on the Trust to hold my experimental wildlife management on course for the foreseeable future, with Michael Swales, whose hand will be on the tiller.

Faith Gadsby has not only coped with the chores of translating my spidery handwritten scrawl to legible typescript, but also contributed shrewd comments on the text.

My sincere thanks are due both to such friends in need and to the countless strangers who I have discovered are equally passionate in their concern for conservation of the environment and rural amenities.

Finally, I dedicate this book with love to Jess, who has shared my pleasures for more than 50 years of happy marriage and been my staunch ally in the black periods of griping worry-guts, when our backs were to the wall in defence of our life's work against the greed of the Leisure Revolution.

PHIL DRABBLE
Goat Lodge, *April 1991*

GORDON BENINGFIELD

Phil Drabble grew up at a time when the countryside had a greater variety of richness, colour and form. I remember him telling me that when he was a boy he could hear the sound of sheep bells as the flocks roamed the downland landscape. His fascination for wildlife and people that lived and worked in the countryside formed a lasting impression which has dominated his life.

Although he spent his early career in industry, where he had great success, his love of the countryside was always the overriding influence.

For a writer and naturalist the natural world offers so much that many people specialize, but for Phil Drabble the whole subject is irresistible. It may be the first butterfly of spring, the sound of birdsong, deer moving through dappled woodland sunlight, the forms created by the long shadows of an autumn day, all this is why he is a passionate conservationist, creating his own nature reserve.

Through his distinguished career as a writer and broadcaster he encourages us all to get out, study and appreciate the natural world but there is always a sound practical side in his approach to the countryside – that of enhancing wildlife habitats.

And so to this autobiography which gives us a rich kaleidoscope of life with his wife Jess, and his continuing concern with the pressures on our environment, above all his growing awareness and faith in the future for wildlife and for us all.

ONE

DERELICTION

The Industrial Revolution, a century and a half ago, shattered our way of life as irrevocably as an atom bomb. I know because I was born and brought up in the Black Country of industrial Staffordshire and learned to take the dereliction of the brave new world for granted.

In the guise of making machines the slaves of Man, to cushion him from hardship and provide prosperity, the new culture created an overwhelming tide of countrymen surging into towns. They were swept, as helpless flotsam, from the rural tranquillity of their ancestors into squalid, overcrowded tenements clustered round factories.

Machines, powered by steam and later by electricity or internal combustion engines, made craftsmen obsolete overnight. They mass-produced cheap counterfeits of products which skill and pride had once made the envy of the world. New roads and railways and canals defiled the unspoiled countryside, but to have cleared up the slovens of such 'enterprise' would have been derided as mere sentimental pandering to memories of the past.

Modern mass-production may require no more than mindless automatons, capable only of pushing buttons in the sequence laid down on an instruction sheet. Such 'workers' – as opposed to crafts-men – are expendable and can be made redundant as easily as a worn-out machine can be scrapped. But folk memory recalls ancestors whose craftsmanship produced true works of art, each individually perfect for its function. Tradition and country sports and the gift of managing animals with inbred stockmanship are still more deeply ingrained in their descendants than greed for profit.

I was bred and born in Staffordshire's Black Country, and I am intensely proud of it, not because of the surroundings, which were squalid, but because of a mutual respect and affection for the friends and neighbours I grew up with. However black my background was, the emphasis was always on country, because the people there were still genuine countrymen at heart. It may have been an unlikely habitat for a young naturalist but an instinctive love of wildlife possessed my soul as a child – and the signs are that it will continue to enrich me to the grave.

My family had contributed more than their quota to the dereliction left by the Industrial Revolution and I believe that the dereliction threatened by the present Leisure Revolution will surpass it unless our generation takes effective steps to stop the rot. So this book is my small contribution towards highlighting the dangers and suggesting ways of making amends for ancestors who sacrificed pride for profit.

My forebears owned a stone quarry at Darley Dale, in Derbyshire, and made their living by tearing the heart out of what is now part of the Peak National Park. Any suggestion that they should restore the landscape they had debauched would have been scorned as trendy for England then took pride in being the Workshop of the World, not its nanny.

Grandfather died in 1898 when my Old Man was only twenty-one, leaving him as head of a family of about five or six boys and three or four girls, so that he had to manage the quarry, to keep the family, until his brothers were self-supporting. He then sold the business and gave the money to his mother.

Signing on as a medical student at the London Hospital at the age of twenty-nine, he qualified at thirty-four and in 1911 joined a practice at Bloxwich, on the edge of Staffordshire's industrial Black Country, as assistant to the local family doctor.

His family dispersed to the four winds and, since we had so little in common, I have never even troubled to discover how many there were. I prefer to choose my friends.

Being a humble assistant he was expected to visit his patients, over a sprawling practice, on a push bicycle because his meagre salary would not stretch to anything grander. His senior partner was driven round by a groom in a splendid, gleaming dog-cart with a high-stepping trotting horse. The Old Man was not easily downtrodden, so he soon scrabbled far enough up the social peck order to make life less arduous – at least in theory! The most vivid of my early memories are of him setting out after morning surgery, in all weathers, to visit his patients on a motorbike.

It was a fearsome contraption, constructed long before the era when 'kick-starters' were invented. The rider had to push the machine and run beside it until he judged he could let in the clutch, to get the engine turning over fast enough to fire. When it sparked and spluttered and coughed into life, the rider had to vault into the saddle at a canter and, with luck and agility, ride off in full control.

I was born in a semi-detached villa on a bend in the main road between Bloxwich and Walsall, and tramcars clanked and rattled past the house from four in the morning till eleven at night. The working day had not then been constricted by trades union regulations so that, when visitors came to stay, they got no sleep after dawn except on Sundays, when the trams didn't start till six o'clock.

The short drive from the house sloped steeply down to the main road, which eased the task of push-starting the bike in gear fast enough to make the engine fire. But great delicacy was required to set the throttle opening exactly right. Too little gas resulted in no more than an asthmatic splutter. Too much made the engine fire so rapidly that the bike took charge and belted off faster than the would-be rider could run. It was the prototype of the infernal combustion engines which help to breach the ozone layer and threaten to ruin our civilization.

It was inevitable that the bike would eventually take control down the drive. The Old Man, who was built more for comfort than for speed, could neither keep up nor jump on so, being a prudent fellow, he let go of the handlebars and left it to its own devices. The engine screamed in premature triumph, crossed the tramlines at a furious pace and telescoped into a heap of worthless scrap iron when it piled, head-on, into the wall of the villa across the road.

Sadly, it did not self-destruct before it had been the cause of a terminal row with our next-door neighbour, who was also our landlord. He had a large mongrel dog, called Turk, which spent so much time chained, in all weathers, to a draughty kennel that he was understandably very evil-tempered. He was also intelligent enough to develop an obsessional hatred of motorbikes in what he regarded as 'his' yard. If he happened to be off the chain when the Old Man wheeled out his iron steed, Turk stood up until the rider was totally involved in pushing it to start. While he was concentrating on gaffering the machine, Turk seized the opportunity to chase him and bite his flailing legs.

The Old Man did not submit to such indignity lightly so, seeing Turk rise to his feet ready to attack, he picked up a 'bibble' (pebble) about as big as a duck egg and launched it at his assailant with all his might. He was a pretty good shot, and the direction was spot-on. Unfortunately the elevation left something to be desired. Instead of landing in the cur's ribs with a satisfying dull thud, the bibble hit the yard between his feet and richocheted through our landlord's window. Explaining that he didn't mean to break the window was no easier when the only excuse was that he'd been aiming at the owner's dog who guarded it!

Although he was an urban coal merchant, our neighbour's ancestors had also been 'real' countrymen and had left traces of their rural culture in his blood. He kept a carthorse, to deliver coal, in a stall in the stable in the yard outside Turk's kennel – and a hunter in the loosebox. Like other Black Countrymen, he preferred sport to making money from a coal round.

There was a grassy paddock outside the yard, where the horses took their ease and, beyond the paddock, hundreds of acres of derelict wasteland created a truly Dickensian landscape. Coal pits had been sunk there, and when the coal was won, the surface of the ground above had sagged in, leaving a random chain of 'swags' (mining subsidence pools) as far as the eye could see. Great spoil heaps – 'pit banks' we called them – punctuated the skyline as memorials to the first industrial litter louts who strove for prosperity, not culture. This local man-made wilderness was 'home' to me.

My Old Man, who was both law-abiding and pragmatic, thought nothing of allowing me to wander off from breakfast to supper, entirely on my own, when no more than ten or twelve years old. Nobody thought about muggers or child molesters seventy years ago. Such depravity was a horror deferred for our effete, permissive society. Victims still merited more sympathy than villains when I was young, because basic rural values demanded codes of conduct which were based on discipline – in the home, at school and on the street. Anyone who robbed with violence or interfered with children would have been flogged with the dreaded cat o' nine tails if convicted. If he had been caught by local Black Countrymen, he would have been lucky to escape emasculation.

Years later, a canal bargee, who had been sentenced to twenty strokes with the cat for robbery with violence, showed a friend of mine his back. I gather the scars were as even and parallel as if it were a sheet of printed graph paper, the pattern of lines stretching from his shoulders to his buttocks. When the thrashing was done, he said, the bloody weals were treated by rubbing in salt, like 'curing' a side of bacon. This had prevented infection and left visible scars as a warning to friends with similar aggressive tendencies. The memory of having salt literally rubbed into his wounds had persuaded the culprit to mend his manners for the rest of his life rather than risk an encore.

So the Old Man allowed me to wander out of the yard after breakfast, to cross the paddock, where the horses grazed, and spend the day on my own. The pools of the wasteland were shallow at the edges and only deepened gradually towards the centre, above the cavity left when the coal below had been mined. It was perfectly safe for youngsters to wade round the edges to catch sticklebacks (or 'Jack Bannocks') and leeches and water beetles, caddis worms and newts. Large areas of blue clay subsoil, churned over by mining, supported no vegetation at all, underlining the cost of ravaging the countryside for coal. Only isolated patches of scrub and rush, reed mace and marsh marigolds, thistle and teasel demonstrated Nature's powers to survive against overwhelming odds. Golden coltsfoot and gorse heralded spring as eloquently there as flamboyant foreign flowers in cultivated gardens.

My Old Man, who had great faith in fresh air for growing lads, employed Elsie, a teenage patient, to take me for longer walks on several afternoons a week. She was a jolly girl whose mirth easily swelled through rhythmic crescendos of flatulent giggles which were incurably contagious. They more frequently originated from prophesies of doom than from conventional sources of merriment.

Great crested newts were then common in the swags which were, as yet, unpolluted by the run-off from poisonous pesticides. Those newts' descendants have now been scheduled as in need of legal protection under the Wildlife and Countryside Act to save them from extinction; in my young days we thought nothing of taking ten or twenty home in a bucket. They were never collected in silence. Elsie feigned stark terror as she bade me take care 'because wet efts [askers] spit fire and kill horses'. My fingers might easily drop off if I touched them, she gasped, rocking on her haunches with mirth as she intoned the threat.

The odd thing was that she was nearer the mark than she realized, for she had harvested a half-truth from the oral traditions of simple country folk, which were still current in the Black Country. At school my more educated school gaffers were less advanced.

Salamanders, which are superficially like newts and belong to the same order, are widely believed to be associated with fire; and St George's dragon adversary, often depicted as a giant newt, is conventionally symbolized with smoke and flames belching from its snarling jaws. Elsie knew nothing about such theories, but she had a superstitious dread of the perils of wet efts which fired her illogical compulsion to catch them.

She was a dab hand with a home-made muslin net, and she proudly presented me with twenty huge, flamboyant crested newts for my eighth birthday, leaving them at the house as a surprise. They certainly surprised the family, because I was so elated that I forgot to cover the aquarium and the whole lot had escaped by breakfast time. They spat no fire, but we came across their mummified corpses for weeks, under the carpet and skirting boards and almost anywhere they could creep in their desperate quest for moisture and food and security.

We had great fun with the survivors, however. Neither my Old Man nor Mother was in the least interested in natural history, but they were wise enough to appreciate that my instinctive fascination with any form of wildlife should be encouraged. It might turn out to be the only gift I had. So I was allowed to keep a goldfish bowl of newts in the centre of the breakfast table.

It was totally unsuitable habitat because it let in light all round the sides, instead of only at the surface, as is the case with natural ponds. My father's medical second nature was to insist on scrupulous hygiene, so that I was made to change the water in the goldfish bowl daily, replacing it with inert but sparkling fluid from the tap. This gave no scope for establishing water plants which normally support the beetles and larvae and other wildlife on which newts feed. Even more important was the fact that water plants form the natural breeding habitat of the species.

Female newts do not lay eggs in amorphous masses like frog spawn, but in strings of individual eggs, like sausages. These dangle below the female in a chain, which grows longer as each egg is expelled, until she can reach down and grasp the end egg between her forefeet. Her instinct then is to break each egg free and conceal it, safe from predators, in the leaf of a water plant growing in the pond. My goldfish bowl was devoid of such necessities so that the newt was driven almost frantic in a hopeless search for suitable concealment for her ever-lengthening string of eggs.

The Old Man, observant as all good diagnosticians are, cracked the problem with clinical detachment. He shredded part of a sheet of newspaper into pieces about the size of confetti and sprinkled the scraps on the surface of the water. The frantic newt grasped them as eagerly as if they had been verdant water weed and proceeded to conceal each of her precious progeny in a plebian newspaper package. The Old Man reckoned it was the best thing he'd seen in the *Mirror* for weeks. The same would be far more true today!

I fed the newts on worms which I dug from the muckheap in the yard, outside our neighbour's stable, but it was not always easy to find small enough quarry. By dropping one or two strong wrigglers into the goldfish bowl before starting breakfast, we were able to watch the newts feed instead of straining to make polite conversation at the one meal where all civilized people are silent.

Even if a worm were too large to be swallowed in comfort, a ravenous newt would grab it and struggle to swallow it. There followed a prolonged battle during which the worm was gradually subdued till it was eventually consumed and disappeared from sight – temporarily. The victor then exhibited signs of acute discomfort, which was obvious because its belly was visibly palpated, from within, by prey which had not yet conceded defeat. Within a minute or so, the victim would wriggle out and reappear, forcing its captor to mount a counter-attack to swallow it again. This could happen three or four times before the writhing worm eventually gave up the ghost, and meanwhile we sat round the breakfast table laying odds on how many bows the unwilling actor would take before the final curtain. It laid the foundations of a lifelong thirst for first-hand anecdotal evidence about the habits of creatures with which I have shared my life much more satisfying than reading about them in boring biology books.

The scrubby vegetation of the 'pitbonks' where I caught my newts supported an astonishing variety of other wildlife. As a child of five or six, I collected devil's coach-horse beetles, gorgeous tiger moths, and dor beetles (or 'Bob Owlers') which zoomed through the dusk in the evenings and hid up under cow pats by day. The poverty-stricken habitat supported nettles, where thrived caterpillars which could be kept and fed in jam jars till they pupated and eventually emerged as peacock butterflies; we knew these as 'King Georges', though their conventional name, Peacocks, was so much more descriptive. Nobody thought of providing me with a decent vivarium, so my captives survived in totally unsuitable cigarette boxes – made to take 100 'gaspers' – or in tins with holes punched through the lids with an old nail.

It was fashionable in those days for lads to make collections of butterflies and moths, pinned out in rows, with wings outstretched as 'naturally' as possible by arranging them before they had been set irrevocably in rigor mortis. Other lads assured me that this was all right 'because insects don't feel pain', so that crucifixion with a pin caused no discomfort! However true that may or may not have been I never swallowed it, and a specialist, who had called at the house to visit one of the Old Man's patients, tried to put my mind at ease by teaching me to make a 'killing bottle', which was, of course, an unheard-of sophistication in my circle of friends! 'Sniffing' solvents for kicks was another unknown eccentricity in my day, but the Old Man would not let me play with chloroform for obvious reasons. So his specialist friend told me to collect laurel leaves, pound them up and put them in a bottle with the insects I wanted to 'set'. My victims would then die peacefully and could be painlessly pinned in whatever attitude I fancied.

Yet I found that equally unattractive, and I can't help feeling that my instinctive sensitivity was a hereditary relic of ancestors who had spent timeless generations in real country – which wasn't Black! I am equally convinced that the present drift from town back to what is left of the countryside is motivated by precisely the same nostalgia for something more deep-seated and wholesome than our present way of life.

Later in the season, when our captive newts had spawned and faded out of their brilliant breeding colours, we returned them to the swags where we had caught them. We often replaced them by equally brilliant sticklebacks and the males of which, in breeding colour, were known as 'butchers', partly because of their gorgeous red bellies and partly because of their natural aggression – which often ended in slaughter.

The reed mace and water iris and a variety of pondweed in the swags was perfect habitat for dragonflies, which Elsie called 'horse stingers' and held in high affection: her prophecy that we should all get stung sent her into more paroxysms of flatulent giggles. They don't sting, of course. What Elsie insisted was their 'sting' is simply the ovipositor, through which they deposit single eggs on the leaves of water plants. These eggs developed into truly fearsome larvae, far more dragonlike than the perfect insects, but children have an instinctive love of pretending to be frightened, as is obvious from the horror stories told by authors of fairy tales and children's books. Despite her total ignorance of technical biology, I reckon that I owe more to Elsie than to any of the pseudo-scientists who stuffed my head at school.

We were not alone in our quest for wildlife in the wasteland behind our house. Black Countrymen, in those days, were natural stockmen. They may have lived in squalid rows of back-to-back houses, with common earth closets in communal yards and one cold tap between a dozen or more houses. The earth closets were emptied into ash-pits – or ess holes – where the dung was mixed with spent ashes from the fires and stored until the 'night soil' men came to collect it while luckier neighbours slept.

It is difficult to be a good stockman under such conditions, with nowhere but a pigsty in the yard and a crowded kitchen to house the stock. So the Old Man's patients, who were also my friends, kept pigeons and raced them from rickety pens in the yards behind the houses, or they trained singing canaries in the front room. The real enthusiasts among them sometimes kept gamefowl too, for cock-fighting was still a common if illicit 'sport' in the area.

These fighting cocks were so aggressive that no more than one could ever be loose at a time, for two would set to and fight to the death. But enthusiasm was such that I knew one chap who kept six gamecocks, one penned in each shelf by the side of the kitchen fireplace. His wife was expected to let them loose, separately, in the yard for an hour at a time, the free one being caught and the next loosed in turn for its period of exercise. This was not as difficult as it might sound, for all the chap's wife had to do to catch the cock at liberty was to lift the next from the cupboard and drop him in the yard. The first one attacked immediately. All that was necessary then was to separate them by picking up the bird which was due for return to the cupboard.

Men with simpler tastes – or less accommodating wives – were often busy round the 'pitbonks' when we went to fish for newts or Jack Bannocks or to collect coltsfoot, wild rose, ladysmocks or other wild flowers. The chaps we saw were often there to catch birds, which they took home to keep in cages, to enliven their own squalid surroundings with bird song fit for the most beautiful and secluded countryside.

Teasels, behind our house, were an irresistible magnet for gold-finches (or 'seven-coloured linnets'). There were flocks of greenfinches (or 'Joeys'), though they were not highly prized because they were neither as beautiful as seven-coloured linnets, nor did they sing as sweetly. Brown linnets, bullfinches and yellowhammers were common in the scrub and people captured these by anointing the thistles and twigs where they perched with birdlime, a foul, sticky substance which stuck to their feathers so that they could be picked off their perches. Birdlime has long since – rightly – been made illegal, and it is now forbidden to catch most wild birds by any other method either.

The more enterprising of the old bird catchers used a decoy bird in a cage to arouse the curiosity of its wild relatives, which came to inspect the fluttering captive or to drive him off their territory. Meanwhile the trapper sat in concealment, some way off, holding the cord to a 'clap' net, which clapped over his victims when he tugged. Scientific ornithologists now use rockets to launch their nets to catch birds for ringing, but I think that is equally unjustified.

Larks were popular cage birds, though I know of no sight more distressing than a lark behind bars, when it should be carolling from on high in the heavens. When a lark's nest was found, it was kept under close observation until the fledglings were almost feathered and within a few days of leaving the nest. A garden riddle was then inverted over nest and young so that the parents could poke food to their chicks through the mesh. It was thus possible to keep them under control for several days after they would otherwise have fledged and dispersed, so that they were far more robust than newly fledged birds would be. The trapper then collected the whole brood, which could be hand-reared at home before being confined, singly, in tiny cages – these used to turn my heart over every time I saw and heard them.

Elsie and I both hated the bird catchers, though in retrospect, I think their cruelty was due to lack of imagination rather than sadism. There was not much we could do about it, for such behaviour was tolerated by society, but we often argued with them and trampled the thistles they had 'laced' with birdlime, and we sometimes freed the captives from their decoy cages or moved riddles from over lark nests. They swore at us and threatened to 'tan our hides', but nobody ever laid a finger on us. I dread to think what would happen to boys and teenage girls who interfered with the activities of modern vandals in such an isolated wilderness. Our 'liberated' and 'progressive' society is now antisocial enough to rate villains higher than victims.

Perhaps one explanation was that our neighbours were still realistic countrymen, at heart, though forced to live in an urban habitat. Modern hoodlums have been bred by several generations of townees and, though migrating, physically, back to the countryside, they have left their minds behind in inner cities.

The contribution towards urban dereliction by my own family, with their quarries in Derbyshire, was matched by that of my in-laws nearer home. They came from farming stock but the grandfather of Jess, my wife, found coal on his land and sunk some small coal pits about 3 miles from where I was born at Bloxwich. The family branched out into iron works and George Thomas, my father-in-law, managed an iron forge at the Birchhills on the edge of the Black Country (where birch trees had, in fact, long been conspicuous by their absence).

Although my father-in-law earned his keep in typical Black Country heavy industry, there was no shadow of doubt that rural tastes, bred in his bones, came out in his blood. He travelled 3 or 4 miles to work each morning on horseback, and kept a couple of hunters at home for his recreation. He also shot and fished, and I used to tease him that I couldn't understand when he made time for any work. But he still retained the physical craftsman's touch of his country forebears and was famous in his works for his skill at getting particles of iron out of workers' eyes, for that was the commonest industrial injury in the forge. He carried, in his waistcoat pocket, a small, superbly smooth, little steel implement, about the size of a toothpick, on which he could roll back eyelids with the greatest delicacy, so that he could remove the smallest, sharpest foreign body as gently as Florence Nightingale.

The sort of medicine my father practised was more a way of life than a means of earning his living. His patients were far more than mere symbols on some receptionist's anonymous card index or computer. Many of them, including the Thomas family, were also our valued family friends. I first met Jess at a family party at their house when I was five. I have always hated any party, and that was no exception, so it was another twenty years before we married, but she still puts up with me cheerfully, though our golden wedding is now well past. We have had a rich and varied life, making scores of pleasant acquaintances and more than our share of close friends. There has never been a period of our lives we would have swapped for the period before because we have enjoyed each, as it came, even more than the last.

It occurred to us one day that the personal memories of our parents and ourselves spanned more than a century of rural change. My father lived to eighty-four and I am over seventy-six, so between us we have actually experienced the changing habitat and ways of life from his young days, in the 1870s, to what is happening now. Add to that the experience of my father's father, passed on by verbal family anecdotes, and our combined 'first-hand' memory goes back well into the Industrial Revolution.

My father-in-law was even older, for he was well into his nineties when he died, born into life on a prosperous farm and flourishing in 'heavy' industry. Jess and I often compare notes to cross-check family evidence harking back to the mass migration, from countryside to towns, forced upon our forefathers when communal factories replaced skilled craftsmanship. The saving grace was that the change was so violent that whole communities often migrated *en bloc*, because the hereditary craftsmanship had sired such dignity and pride that there was deep pleasure in belonging to a small, creative community which was rightly confident that it was unsurpassed at its own traditional trade. This was still obvious in Staffordshire's Black Country right up to the end of the last war, despite the fact that centralized power controlled factories.

For instance, some of the best saddlers and harness makers in the world had settled in Walsall, which was justly famous for its leather goods. The saddlers needed satellite trades to make stirrups, bits, buckles and similar leather 'hardware', and Bloxwich, my own home, was as famous for very highly specialized 'light' blacksmiths' wares as Walsall was for leather – not only for stirrups and bits, in steel, but also for brass plates, studs and buckles, for dog collars, steel awls for the leather makers and probably the last steel spurs for fighting cocks. These were illegal in my youth, but still compared with 'Tepin' spurs, made at Bloxwich in the 1700s, which are now fetching a mint of money in the antique trade – not always to be put on show as ornaments, they say!

The Black Country itself it about 18 miles across, from Bloxwich to Stourbridge, or Smethwick to Wolverhampton. When I was growing up, it still comprised a number of highly individual towns, each with its own trade, the specialist craftsmen – or their ancestors – having come as a whole, viable community from the surrounding countryside. Each town was intensely proud of its own specialist trade. The inhabitants were as territorial as badgers, and were fired by intense local patriotism, while they rightly believed – and were prepared to prove – that no other craftsman were as good at their particular trade.

The Stourbridge area was – and is – world famous for the quality of its glass, though the best quality was made in Wordsley and Brierly Hill and what were surrounding villages.

Strangers visiting the area up to the end of the last war could not fail to notice in the strong local dialect the sing-song lilt of Wales. Presumably when the tide of immigrants was set flowing by the Industrial Revolution, the Stourbridge area was populated by immigrants from Wales, who arrived and settled together as a community.

Cradley Heath is famous for forged chains, from the light links required for harness or lifting tackle, to gigantic links, weighing several hundredweight apiece, which were forged for anchor chains on ocean-going liners.

Gornal had a community of itinerant salt hawkers, who collected salt by the truck load from Droitwich or Stafford, and distributed it, each with his pony and costermonger's flat. I once did a broadcast there and arranged to meet Harry Watton. When I arrived, I was told that there were over thirty hawkers named Watton, several of them Harry, and was therefore asked if I knew his nickname. I didn't know, so we didn't meet, though I was told later that the chap I wanted couldn't have come that day anyway because he was up before the Beak on a charge of poaching his neighbour the Earl of Dudley's pheasants! I imagine the police would also have had difficulty in pinning the right Watton down, as such multiplicity of the same surname must have facilitated getting a credible alibi. But the fact that he – and plenty of other Black Countrymen – were such skilled poachers hammered home the fact of their rural background.

Bill Swingewood, a glass maker from Brierley Hill, was also a real artist with a catapult, or 'flirter' as he called it. He once told me (in a live broadcast!) that he 'liked to get his pheasants agin the moon'. Shooting pheasants at night is considered a bit eccentric in our neck of the woods, especially with a 'flirter', so I asked him if he was often knocked off for poaching. 'No,' he reflected. 'Never. I've shot with Lord Dudley for over twenty years – but he's never found out!'

Those who talked of 'a' Black Country accent before the war simply did not know the Black Country. There was a different accent, and often a different dialect, for every Black Country town. Sing-song Cradley Heath, gruff Gornal, and far more northern Walsall were all as different as chalk from cheese, because each of them retained the specific quality of the area from which the town had grown during the Industrial Revolution. We only had to hear a stranger open his mouth and we knew at once which local town he came from.

The hawkers from Gornal did not only take salt to sell. They took 'lily-white sond' (or sand) as well, which they sold to the womenfolk to scour their front steps. It was symptomatic of the spirit of the place to be clean however poor you were. In any inner city – even in those days – there was squalor and litter and the filth that seems to be unavoidable when masses of strangers are herded together. The tendency is to sink to the level of the lowest common denominator.

Countryfolk, who all know each other personally, have great professional pride. They strive for craftsmanship which is better, not so much than their neighbours' work, but certainly better than any rivals' from another area. By the same token, they liked their houses to be not necessarily better than their neighbours', nor more valuable, but more respectable. At the very least they were determined not to let the side down. I still see the same spirit in my work as a rural writer. Countryfolk see nothing old hat about dignified self-respect.

So the men from Gornal sold lily-white sand, to scour front door steps till there was not a spot nor a scar nor a blemish on them. Whoever walked down a street of craftsmen's cottages on a Sunday would not only find superb works of art, made by the householder or his family, in front rooms; they would see equal pride in the way the houses were kept. It was not the shallow 'keeping up with the Joneses' but determination to maintain their own standards.

Despite the crowded streets of my boyhood, the deep-seated love of the soil ensured that gardening was still as compulsive as it had been when great-grandfathers plodded behind the plough. Any odd corners among the industrial dereliction would be snapped up for allotments, not only to feed the family but also to grow produce to enter in local shows which would establish who could grow the longest carrot or most luscious tomato or biggest leek. Rural trade secrets of just how such feats could be accomplished were still regarded as inviolate, to be guarded with the keeper's life. Some of them were so far-fetched that they sounded ridiculous, yet investigation left a lingering suspicion that there might be something in them.

One old chain maker was justly famous for growing bigger and better chrysanthemums than any rival. Being no gardener and therefore no threat as a competitor, I asked him to tell me his secret. Rather to my surprise, he promised to tell me provided I would swear, by everything he and I regarded as sacred, that I would not tell anyone – until he was dead. It was a promise nothing would have induced me to break. After considerable theatrical looking over shoulders and round the room, in case of eavesdroppers, he eventually let the cat out of the bag.

'I send the missus round the neighbours,' he said, 'to collect the chamber-lie from any woman who is pregnant, and I water the plants with that. You would be surprised how they grow:'

I would! I wrote it off as mumbo-jumbo superstition, but mentioned it years after the old boy died to a close friend who was a professor and principal at a foremost veterinary college. My friend thought it no joke at all because he had recently read a scientific paper on the advantages of using the hormones in the urine of pregnant mares for growing bulbs. Subsequently my friend dug out some obscure research about tests for pregnancy in the time of the pharaohs. Apparently the Egyptians took seven grains of wheat (a magical number) and watered them with the urine of the girl supposed to be in the family way. They took another seven grains from the same sample and watered them with urine of a woman past her menopause. If both samples grew evenly, the girl was not pregnant. If the girl's sample outstripped that of the woman who could not be pregnant, the girl was in the family way. My professor friend and I were still sceptical but, since that time, tests have been developed using rabbit urine which seem to confirm the theory for girls who may have been more friendly than careful.

We wondered how this totally obscure bit of ancient Egyptian folklore could possibly have been passed down to an unlettered old Black Countryman, long before modern science had stumbled on it. The possible explanation lies in the communal earth closets in bitterly cold common courtyards. It would have been unavoidable to go across the yard to the closet for complete evacuation – but far more comfortable to use a chamber pot for urination in the warmth of the bedroom, and then to slop out in the morning. It might have been more trouble than it was worth to go all the way to the earth closet for that and far easier to skim it out of the back door, across the yard. The grass and weeds would grow, but when Mum was in the family way the rate of growth would increase. And gardeners competent enough to produce bigger and better onions than their rivals are surely as capable of putting two and two together as either ancient Egyptians or modern scientists!

The instinctive, dogged determination to cling to country ways even in overcrowded towns was not confined to working folk. Our curate, the Revd Davis, was a rawboned, ruddy man with the gait of a ploughman, accustomed to plodding the furrows his forebears' horses created. It was easier to visualize him hoeing turnips than spellbinding his congregation from a pulpit.

As a child I was rather frightened of him, through a stupid misunderstanding. The Old Man was a church warden, and the new curate had a reputation for sharing my interests, so soon after he came I was sent round to his lodgings to take tea with him. We were both rather shy and embarrassed so, to break the ice, he said that he had heard I was fond of dogs. 'I had a marvellous dog called Pat,' he said. 'He was an Irish terrier. I was very fond of him.'

He reached across, opened a cupboard door by my chair, and there, mounted like a fox's mask, was poor Pat's head, to keep his memory green! It nearly nipped our friendship in the bud.

Many real countrymen are pretty unimaginative. They have to be, to spend endless energy rearing stock and then assigning the fruit of their labours to the abattoir. But the Revd Davis's nostalgia for the life of his ancestors was clearly overwhelming. When his father died he left him his hunter, and it was the apple of the son's eye. He was often seen, at six in the morning, before early service, scything the churchyard to reap fodder for the horse. There was a seedy little smallholding among the spoil heaps behind our house, and the curate not only persuaded the owner to find lodgings for his hunter – in an old bull pen – but also to allow him to keep his own cow there. So he was able to collect his 'own' milk daily and, whenever he could leave his clerical duties long enough, he milked his cow as well. It was a satisfying, sensual link with a pleasanter past and also broke common ground with his parishioners which was far more personal than could be achieved by conventional witness.

I can just remember being carried out, as a toddler in 1917, to see the searchlights when a German Zeppelin bombed Walsall and killed the mayoress. It was said that the victim was herself a Hun by birth, who had married an Englishman. 'Justice,' our friends said, 'was seen to be done!'

That was about the only local damage from enemy action during the First World War, but the congestion and potential capacity for munitions made the area a tempting target between 1939 and 1945. The real change did not come till after the Second War when there was a national drive to repair the ravages of air raids and at the same time to sweep away the back-to-back slum property created during the Industrial Revolution. So a publisher invited me to write a book about the Black Country, since I had lived and worked there all my life. I loved my fellow Black Countrymen and shared their instinctive loyalty to rural ways, however unattractive technology had made the habitat. It should have been a pleasure to record the rehabilitation of people and places which had been the casualties of a century of 'progress'. Sadly, it turned out to be a thumbnail sketch of the moment of terminal disruption.

The task of rehousing was left to bureaucratic professional planners, who may have been wizards on the technical construction of buildings but appear to have been wimps when it came to dealing with the people who were condemned to live in them. Parasitic speculative developers jumped in on the act to maximize profit, at whatever cost to society and the environment. Some rogue or fool added insult to injury by dreaming up the nightmare of high-rise flats, which could confine the greatest number of people in the smallest physical space. The other ploy was to choose an area in which a friendly developer had got, or could get, a financial stake and to grant planning permission for a new 'estate' of mass-produced council houses, from which the developer could make even more money and, hopefully, see that his chums on the council would not be out of pocket. The novel term of 'estate' for such excrescences was the only concession to the rural origins of the hapless inhabitants.

However, jerry-built as most of them were, there is no doubt that the new council houses were a vast improvement on the back-to-back slums they replaced. They had indoor sanitation, small gardens of their own, electricity or gas and no common courtyards.

The stupidity was that individuals were rehoused wherever there happened to be a vacancy instead of whole communities being moved, *en bloc*, as social groups, which could have retained the personality of the villages from which their ancestors were torn. Big Brother, at the town hall, thought he knew better, shuffling local populations as mindlessly as a pack of cards. Each family could fetch up in unfamiliar surroundings, cheek by jowl with perfect strangers, as indifferent to neighbours they didn't even know as the characterless masses in any inner city.

My publisher's offer to commission the book resulted in an eye-witness record of the Black Country at the moment of its disintegration by petty bureaucrats, parish-pump politicians and those who consort with them. Instead of creating a new series of communities, each retaining its own well-merited pride, where discipline and behaviour are maintained by the pressure of public opinion, the planners set the seeds of our present lawless lot, where anything goes because 'who cares what the neighbours think, if you don't even know who your neighbours are?'

Nobody who knows the area can doubt the scale of dereliction left by the Industrial Revolution. But the physical damage to the landscape could have been far worse if the codes of conduct of those who were forced to live there had not been disciplined by craftsmen's pride and by the instinct not to let one's friends and neighbours down.

Our current technological revolution is much more ruthless. There is the gut-gnawing stress of imminent redundancy, for nobody knows whether his firm may be the helpless victim of a take-over when he awakes tomorrow. Such fears are magnified by the prospect of a by-pass appearing in the back garden overnight or some horrific 'theme park' on the horizon. The resulting insecurity breeds an overwhelming nostalgia for the old-fashioned values of tradition, and physical skills, basic stockmanship and neighbours we have always known. Privacy and seclusion and the continuity implied by visions of communing with wildlife and revelling in birdsong are vital priorities. A cottage in the country, with personal friends as neighbours, suddenly matters more than the most prestigious status symbols of our acquisitive society.

Many such daydreams may turn out to be nostalgic moonshine, where the substance falls far short of the shadow. Nonetheless, the fact is that an inevitable result of our shifty world is an irresistible tide of people migrating in the opposite direction to trends during the Industrial Revolution. This time, instead of being forced by circumstances beyond their control to leave countryside they love for towns they hate, whole populations are moving back from towns to the countryside. The only way to secure the best of both worlds for the future is to take adequate steps to prevent greed and corruption exploiting what should be the rural heritage of generations yet to come.

TWO

GROWING PAINS

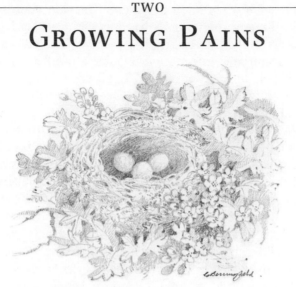

My first bout of worry guts griped me at the age of nine, though I was lucky enough to avoid a second attack till the next wave hit me well past my mid-seventies. (Worry guts, the killer disease of our technological age, is just another term for stress. It is the motivating force which drives tens of thousands of city dwellers back to the countryside in an often vain search for wholesome values, continuity and tradition, and above all security.)

Stress is not only engendered by the prospect of possible redundancy or the physical disturbance of home or surroundings. My Worry Guts struck me down, as a nine-year-old, when my mother died. I was a boarder at prep school at the time, and my only chinks of light were periodic visits home at half-term or for school holidays. The parting, when I had to go back to school, was as traumatic for my mother as it was for me, because she was deeply affectionate but over-protective. Her nightmare was that I would think that she had simply abandoned me.

This may sound incomprehensible to parents now, for modern schools have easier discipline, less bullying and more comforts than were common when I was there. I remember that, before my first term, when I was only eight years old, my Old Man warned me that I should find boys at school who were older and larger and would bully me if I let them. The advice he gave was simple and practical. 'If you see a bigger boy about to bully you,' he said, 'don't wait till he starts. Punch him on the nose, as hard as you possibly can. He'll find someone else to bully!' It was original theory of the pre-emptive strike which now dominates international politics, and it served me very well, if it did little for my popularity. I still use the principle, with my pen rather than with my fists, when I feel threatened.

The school in which I was incarcerated was at Edgbaston, a suburb of Birmingham, where the grounds supported a surprising variety of wildlife, from grey squirrels (or 'tree rats') to songbirds and butterflies and moths. It is obvious to anyone who flies over the suburbs of any large town that they are potentially superb nature reserves because there is such a wide range of habitat to support a rich variety of species. Manicured lawns and trim flower beds adjoin dense bushes and thick hedges, ideal for nesting cover. Berried shrubs supply, food while the huge range of flowers attracts butterflies and moths. There was always something of interest, if only I could escape from class or organized games (both of which I hated) and from my rowdy schoolmates, with whom I had little in common, because I am, by nature, a loner. I cracked the problem by sneaking out of my dormitory at first light to wander round the garden and playing fields, collecting caterpillars – which I kept to pupate in jam jars – searching for birds' nests or simply listening to the dawn chorus, which had delighted countless generations of my rural ancestors.

The sudden death of my mother made the bottom drop out of this world. What security my imagination had managed to conjure up evaporated overnight. I felt totally alone and deserted.

I had, of course, never heard the expression Worry Guts, but I soon learned the meaning the hard way. When I escaped to the privacy of my own bed, I could not sleep. My bowels turned to belly-rotting water and I was griped by spasms of physical nausea which gave a foretaste of the stress experienced by so many of my contemporaries now, who suddenly realize that their own lives have drifted out of control. They find that they have been chucked on the scrap heap or forced to up sticks and move to less congenial surroundings and that the home they have slaved out their guts to acquire is suddenly in the path of the chunnel or a supermarket or is otherwise worthless.

To a sensitive, imaginative child of nine, the shock was over-whelming, and my reaction was the same as that of so many adult victims of our modern curse of insecurity. I turned, instinctively, to the deep well of wholesome rural values which were secure and safe for so many generations. I began to sneak out of my dormitory even earlier in the morning to rub shoulders in the gardens with wildlife which had been there before the city or suburbs were built. The sense of continuity was very comforting.

But it so happened that I was an imaginative as well as a sensitive child. For the first and last time in my life I saw a ghost, and the memory is as vivid now as it was when I first saw it almost seventy years ago. There was a very large, pollarded oak on the corner of the playing field, with a short, stubby trunk twice the diameter of a telephone kiosk. As I walked towards it, in the half-light, I thought I saw a trap door open, through which my mother stepped out to reassure me all was well. It had the reverse effect, because I was terrified by my own imagination, and I looked like death at breakfast time.

Luckily for me, my headmaster was both observant and wise. He must have known that I was in the habit of playing truant from my dormitory, but instead of disciplining me, he had appreciated that solitude was the therapy I needed. So he had allowed me to wander, undisturbed – but far from undetected.

When he realized that something was seriously amiss, he got up early himself, came upon me 'accidentally' when I was distressed and gently questioned me. I blurted out the whole story about my mother appearing from a trap door in the oak, and he said nothing to ridicule it. Some of the oafs who were subsequently responsible for my education would have told me to pull myself together and get back to bed, probably with a sore backside to drive the lesson home. Not so the headmaster of my prep school. He and I examined the tree trunk minutely, as if he really shared my conviction that it contained a secret trap door. When neither of us could find evidence to justify my romantic phantasy, he explained what 'real' naturalists would do in such circumstances: they would test my theories scientifically.

So we solemnly went back to his study to collect a reel of black cotton, which we tied firmly but inconspicuously round the tree trunk. Neither my mother nor anyone else, he explained, could open the trap door without breaking the invisible thread tied round it. At dawn next morning we went out to see if the trap door had opened – which, of course, it had not. 'Perhaps,' he suggested gently, 'you have let your heart rule your head. Good naturalists always test their theories scientifically.'

It was a lesson I never forgot. A lifelong interest in wildlife has been enriched because I enjoy finding facts for myself, and checking them objectively, instead of relying solely on the research, theories and press hand-outs of others. My job as a writer has been helped because I can give factual, anecdotal accounts of what I have experienced. It makes competing with those who have to rely on the regurgitated material of others that much easier.

Nor shall I forget the debt I owe to that far-sighted school gaffer, who left his cane in the cupboard when I was out of bounds and eased the numbing terror and stress which I was suffering. It set the seal on a fruitful love affair with the creatures which share the countryside with me.

The other therapy for my stress was the gift of Mick, the first canine love of my life. My yearning for a dog had been as instinctive as my empathy with wildlife, but I had never been allowed one because a semi-detached house, without an inch of garden and fronting a busy main road, had not seemed the ideal home for one. When Mother died, the Old Man relented and stumped up 10 shillings (50p) for a pup out of a pretty little fox terrier bitch belonging to a patient. Nobody knew what the sire had been but, judging by the size and ugliness of my pup's head, the bitch had probably had a street accident with a bull terrier. Both mother and son had a brown patch over one eye and I subsequently became widely known as 'the kid as belongs the lemon-eyed bitch', although it was the dog to which I really 'belonged' though both mother and son were famous locally for their skills at catching rats. We called my pup Mick and he was my shadow for the next ten years·or so and no lad ever had a more faithful dog. It is, of course, quite common now to prescribe the company of a dog as therapy for stress and loneliness, but Mick was sweet medicine long before his time and I owe him far more than he ever owed me.

My public school provided another nasty jolt. There really were bullies there and unpleasant initiation ceremonies similar to those sometimes in the news when any recruits are maltreated in the army. The saving grace, so far as I was concerned, was the school natural history society, popularly known as 'the Bug Soc.'. The man in charge, who was also my housemaster, was an eccentric old bachelor called Bobby. This had no connection with his real name, which was E. H. Furness. The name Bobby arose through the circuitous irrational logic of schoolboys. My housemaster liked and expected to be addressed as Mister Furness, to which he responded by being excessively well mannered and polite. He took pride in never giving commands but in asking for things to be done, prefacing every request by 'Please do this' or 'Please do not do that'. He soon became known as 'the Please-man' – or Bobby for short! The derivation would have given Cockney rhyming slang a high rating in Mensa by comparison.

Bobby was immensely proud of having been educated at Eton, took pride in being immaculately dressed, and his most obvious eccentricity was a nervous, audible sucking of air through his moustache when harrassed by the boys. He was a Greek scholar and had not come to terms with imperial weights and measures, far less with the metric mumbo-jumbo and Common Market currency now force-fed in schools. He never got past Greek numbers so, when administering a beating, he never gave his victim 'six of the best', but contented himself with five.

As a dedicated natural historian, Bobby was also a keen gardener and, unfortunately for us, his flower beds were immediately beneath our dormitory (or 'bedder') window. On warm summer nights, if we continued to talk after lights-out when Bobby was still weeding his flower beds, he would come storming upstairs and, assuming that *everybody* in the bedder had been talking, waste no time on inquests but proceed to give us five each – his beloved Greek pentad – to encourage us to keep quiet.

Five hard strokes from a whippy stick about as thick as a walking stick are far from pleasant, especially when the victim is wearing only pyjamas. I couldn't punch him on the nose, as my Old Man might have suggested, so the only course was to outwit him. I collected a large bag of weed seeds, sifted out of clean grain by the threshing machine when it called on a local farmer, and I sowed poor Bobby's rockery, which was at the far end of his garden. It is one of the few exploits at school of which I am truly ashamed because we really had so much in common – but it certainly worked. Next summer the rockery was a riot of poppies and buttercups, thistle and kedlock, and all the weeds of corn crops before chemists invented foul brews to wipe them out. We had no further trouble for talking after lights-out because the poor chap was totally engrossed in weeding his rockery, well out of earshot. Perhaps this was a good thing, because I am sure the Greeks had a word for such unexpected plagues which certainly would have been out of place in our curriculum!

The Bug Soc. supplied about my only happy memories at school, despite my treachery to its president, and the first money I ever earned from writing was the prize – 7 shillings and 6d (37½p)! – for a Bug Soc. competition for essays in natural history. I scooped the kitty – such as it was – for an essay on protective colouration, which contained quite a lot of original observation, and I won the second prize of 5 shillings (25p) for another essay on falconry, which was almost entirely cribbed from the *Encyclopaedia Britannica*. I have never even owned a hawk!

We were allowed to take nestling jays and magpies and jackdaws from the nest and hand-rear them on bread and milk and scraps scrounged from the school cook. We kept our birds in a disused shed in the garden, where Bobby held regular daily inspections to check that we were looking after them properly and to give most helpful and practical advice if there were any difficulties. He was as enthusiastic about such pets as we were.

But best of all were expeditions to local woods, where trusting owners made free of their lands for our visits.

We had very strict codes of conduct which members of the society themselves enforced. Collecting birds' eggs was perfectly legal in those days – and was still socially acceptable. Intensive husbandry and chemical pesticides have wreaked far more havoc since than all the small boys who went egg collecting before the boffins were let loose. The basic competitive collector's instinct was a powerful incentive, and whoever found a nest was bound, by the society convention, to declare its whereabouts and whether or not an egg had been taken. There was an inviolate rule that no more than one egg was ever taken from a clutch. As a result, I think we did no harm and, in the process, we formed a nucleus of knowledgeable young naturalists who have since worked to leave the countryside as good as, or better than, we found it. We were the foundation for subsequent objective protection campaigners, who despise modern, counter-productive, way-out activists.

The fringe benefits for me were not to be sneezed at. I could get permission to be absent from the organized games I detested to wander, alone and unsupervised, in woodlands up to 5 or 6 miles from the school. My forays were not very sophisticated, by modern academic standards, but I went out into the country to enjoy it because I genuinely loved it, not to write some obtuse tract that would confuse rarity with obscurity. I would have been as bored then by the eternal population surveys and censuses of modern trendy boffins as I am now.

When Bobby retired, a younger, more scientifically orientated biology master took his place but, by our yardstick, he wasn't in the same league. He prattled endlessly on about 'projects' and 'investigations', which might have been acceptable in school hours but were far too boring for our own spare time. We wanted only to enjoy the countryside and the wildlife which shared it, not to make a chore of it.

With the cruel accuracy of earthy schoolboys, we nicknamed him Bunny – because he looked and bred like a rabbit – so there was not much love lost between us. He eventually took what I considered an unfair advantage of me.

I ragged him remorselessly, always keeping just within the letter, if not the spirit, of the law, so that for a long time he could find no legitimate reason to punish me. Then one day someone turned up with one of the typical puerile schoolboyish jokes which are earthy without being coarse enough to give real offence. It was a simple address, which I wrote on an envelope: 'Miss Mary Kepes, The Cockwell Inn, Tillit, Herts. Everybody giggled as it was passed round the class and I forgot all about it. Unfortunately the last boy to receive it left it on a desk, where Bunny found it and recognized my handwriting.

If he had sent for me and given me six, I should have accepted it with good grace as a fair cop, which was entirely my own fault. But he said nothing about it to me, instead passing the 'evidence' to the headmaster, and the first I knew was that I was summoned to his study. He was a weedy little man, with a head too big for his body. He eventually became a bishop and his one accomplishment was the administration of a beating. He was left-handed, with no rhythm, so that it was difficult to tighten the buttock muscles at precisely the right instant to minimize the bite as his stick sunk in. He had the reputation of fetching blood with four strokes, so that the conventional maximum six was a severe ordeal.

Apparently he considered that my crime in recording the whereabouts of the mythical Miss Kepes merited unconventional severity, for he announced his intention of giving me ten. Being the first boy to 'score' over six was about my only distinction at school. As a result I had to report to Letty Lonsdale, the matron, for the next fortnight to have my bottom dressed in her surgery. She was always kind to me and was intensely curious to know what heinous crime I had committed to merit such a thrashing, so she eventually wheedled it out to me.

'Silly boy,' she said. 'Serves you right.' Pause. 'Never leave incriminating evidence about!'

Letty was a very distinguished lady who laid claims to being an aristocrat because she was a cousin of Lord Lonsdale! She had a soft spot for me because I was a naturally insubordinate rebel and we became good friends while she was recovering from a severe bout of pneumonia, which was often fatal in days before antibiotics became a standard treatment. The doctors had applied medicinal leeches to her temple to relieve the pressure and, when she was well enough to take note of her surroundings, the sight of leeches disporting themselves in the 'leech bottle' by her bedside nauseated her. 'Give them to Drabble,' she commanded. 'He will probably like them!'

Bunny was obstructive when I asked permission to keep them in his biology lab, but he could hardly refuse when I pointed out that Miss Lonsdale was still critically ill – and it might prove to have been her last wish to bequeath them to Drabble. I couldn't get them to feed but he insisted that 'leeches feed on blood. Your blood would do, I expect.' As he omitted to tell me how to apply them, I used my own initiative.

The whole class stopped work to watch the experiment as I liberated a leech on the palm of my hand. The prospect didn't appeal to it, so it explored the inside of my forearm, fetching up over the vein half-way between my wrist and elbow. It dug in deep and the blood pulsated down, causing its lower end to swell to the shape of a miniature Indian club. I was objectively interested, the class was delighted, but Bunny got cold feet. 'Get it off, Drabble,' he ordered. 'You've lost more than enough blood.' I tugged at the leech, but it simply stretched like elastic without any sign of letting go. Eventually I pinched its head with a pair of foreceps, forcing it to fall off – but the bleeding didn't stop.

Three hours later I was sent to the doctor who diagnosed a punctured vein, which he proceeded to stitch up. He explained that the proper way to apply a leech is to put it in a test tube and place the mouth of the tube over a patch of skin which does not contain a large vein or artery, so that a tourniquet can be applied if bleeding does not cease.

'Whoever told you to allow the beast to wander at will?' he enquired.

'Mister Littleton,' I replied.

'Then tell Mister Littleton, from me, that he's a bloody fool,' he said.

The temptation, of course, was too great. I waited for a lull in class and raised my arm to speak. On being asked what I wished to say, I passed on the medical man's message, verbatim, to everyone else's delight.

The incident taught me another important fact of life. It can be unwise to try to beat the system without taking adequate precautions against painful consequences. Bunny bided his time for an excuse to send me to the headmaster – and I still have a scar on my forearm to remind me of the cause of the operation.

With the exception of a few wets, most boys were beaten from time to time and, provided it was a 'fair cop', we took it in our stride. This one probably did me good because I didn't count it as a fair cop, and I thought it was over the top for a puerile joke which may have been crude but certainly was not evil. It toughened me up, and I confided to the wise old matron that I would get my own back before I left, for it happened in my last term. So, on my last night, at 4 am, I crept out of the bedder and down to the headmaster's study, which had a private loo attached. I took a tin of home-made 'itching powder', which I had produced in the lab by grinding glass test tubes to fine dust with a pestle and mortar, and sprinkled it round the headmaster's loo seat. The headmaster spoke at assembly before we broke up and the picture of him scratching first one buttock and then the other, as a totally subconscious reflex, will remain among my treasured memories. He had no idea why he was scratching. We had.

My last act before leaving was to call on Letty in her surgery to thank her for her kindness over the past.

'You said you were going to get your own back for that beating,' she said. 'Did you?'

'Yes, Matron, I did,' I replied laconically.

'I thought so,' she said. 'I noticed him scratching during Assembly. Perhaps he will call for treatment, when you have gone. It will be my pleasure to diagnose the cause.'

One of our extra-mural activities, under the umbrella of the Bug Soc., were expeditions with Thorn, the school dog. He was a large collie Airdale cross and one of my regular chores, while doul (or 'fag') to the head boy, was to collect Thorn each evening and deliver him to the housemaster's study.

As well as being large, Thorn was very short-tempered because, if he had been at the beck and call of any boy who wanted him, his life would not have been his own. He therefore resented my command to come and left me in no doubt that he had no intention of being messed around. Not suffering fools gladly, either human or canine, I grabbed his collar and yanked him to his feet. My forearm still carries the scars where he bit me. Deeming discretion the better part of valour, I left him and called on the cook to scrounge some scraps of meat to soft-soap poor Thorn into my study. There I gently muzzled him with a bootlace tied round his muzzle and gave him a hiding he never forgot. Thereafter he accepted me as pack leader, we got on fine, and we enrolled him as the only quadruped to be an honorary member of the Bug Soc. so that he would join us on our expeditions.

Ratting has always been my favourite sport, so we took Thorn along the local streams and encouraged him to 'mark' any rats occupying the holes in the banks. I hadn't got a ferret because Bunny wouldn't let me keep one, so we improvised an extremely effective method of making the rats bolt from their holes. We took with us an iron bar, about as long as a walking stick and of slightly smaller diameter. After driving this into the ground amongst a concentration of tunnels, we thumped the bar repeatedly with a hammer. The bar responded to the blows by reverberating and sending strident shock waves through the area which the rats found insufferable and so bolted into the water. Thorn had a field day and we often bagged half a dozen or more rats in the course of an afternoon.

There were also water hens along most of the streams near school – and Thorn was anything but steady to them. We always claimed it was an 'accident' when he caught one, but we stuffed it in a pocket and took it back to our study where we skinned it, basted it with butter and cooked it in a biscuit tin over a spirit stove. Compared to conventional school tack, it was five-star grub, and that ratting added the traditional countryman's love of sport to our pleasure in the countryside.

The fact that I had established unquestioned pack leadership over Thorn when he bit me had an interesting fringe benefit. Having more than met his match with me, Thorn accepted my dominance and treated me with respect. If I annoyed him, he would roll back his lips, bare his fangs and snarl ferociously, but he knew – and I knew – that it was only bluff: the other boys did not. They respected my natural 'way with dogs' – and I exploited it. One boy, who was larger and older than me, used to bully me a bit till one day I called Thorn, held him by the collar and 'set' him on my tormentor. There was no way he would have attacked, but nobody else knew that. So I trod on his front foot, which made him snarl and growl furiously – at me. Nobody else knew that either. They thought he was out for blood and that only my firm hand on his collar restrained him. I had no more trouble from bully boys who saw the phoney exhibition.

Having been closely involved in television sheep dog trials for many years, I have no doubts about the capacity of dogs for forming a truly telepathic relationship with their master. Shepherds alone with their dogs in the solitude of wild hills become so mentally attuned to their companions that many sheep dog trials are lost not because of any fault of the dog, but because the shepherd gets flustered and his mental indecision is quite obviously passed to the dog.

I have often noticed a similar relationship between two dogs. I had a marvellous German short-haired pointer called Tick which shared my life for twelve years and she used to find – and 'point' – at all sorts of wildlife in my woodland reserve, without doing it any harm. She 'came to the point' at birds' nests, or squatting rabbits, 'jugging' pheasants or new-born deer fawns. There were few living secrets lying hidden in the wood from her, and she always shared them with me. But she had this same telepathic relationship with Belle, my Alsatian, because Belle knew when Tick came to a point, even if she couldn't see her. She would sometimes 'point' – perfectly silently – at a pheasant on eggs or a rabbit in a form (or 'sit') when Belle was the other side of a steep bank or other solid barrier. But wherever she was, Belle *knew* when Tick came to the point and immediately came to investigate.

Thorn went one stage further. He hated cats and killed them if he could. There was a lovely old mulberry tree in the garden outside my housemaster's house, with a huge horizontal branch about 6 feet from the ground. It was said that Thorn once killed a cat which tried to escape by climbing the mulberry tree, though I never discovered how true the story was. Whatever basis there was for the tale, it was an obvious fact that there was no bark on the underside of that horizontal branch, head-high above the garden path. On summer evenings Thorn would go out and leap, roaring with fury, at the underside of the branch, biting at the bark till he eventually collapsed, frothing and slavering, red-eyed and panting, on the ground below. Scientists would scoff that it is anthropomorphic to believe that Thorn could see the ghost of 'his' cat, squatting in safety just out of reach. Perhaps it is no more likely than my fancied trap door in the oak trunk in my prep school garden. I know good countrymen who would at least give Thorn the benefit of the doubt!

In school holidays I struck up an incongruous friendship with Hairy Kelly, a local ratcatcher who made his living actually *catching rats* – how much more dignified than simply laying poison bait for anything suicidal enough to eat it, as is the habit of modern 'rodent operatives'. Their skill is limited to the ability to scatter pre-packed sachets of baited poison where clients tell them rats have been seen. Hairy used ferrets and his hands. He was such a good naturalist that he seemed able to think like a rat, because he could size up the infested habitat and predict which way his quarry would bolt when he introduced his ferrets. He would then place himself between the rats and their escape and literally scoop them up as they tried to pass him.

This was not so difficult for Hairy as for men with more conventional figures. He was a stocky little man, with immensely long arms which would not have seemed out of place on an orang-utan. His great hands hung down at knee level. He also had the reflexes of a test wicket keeper, so that no fugitive seemed to take him by surprise. As fast as the rats were bolted by the ferrets, he scooped them up and stuffed them down his shirt, where they seemed to settle as if the space between his shirt and belly were home-from-home. (He did wear a belt to prevent them slipping lower down his person than might be comfortable!) There the rats were stored till there was a lull in the action, when Hairy retrieved them and tied them safely in a sack. He took this to his 'local' at night where he sold them as 'live rats' to train pups or for competitions to see whose dog could kill ten or twenty faster than his competitors.

When I went ratting with Hairy I used to take along my lemon-eyed terrier Mick, who would bag too much quarry for Hairy's liking. Mick's catches didn't live long enough to see the inside of the rat-catcher's shirt, so he really tolerated my presence only because I gave him a spurious air of respectability. Being a little light-fingered, he was not always welcome where he had been before if rats were not the only things missing when he'd gone. When he met that kind of sales resistance he rubbed his palms ingratiatingly, oozed an oily smile and said, 'Oh, let me come, sir. I've got the doctor's son with me – and I promised to show him how to go on!' At the age of twelve or thirteen 'the doctor's son' knew far more about how to go on than was strictly legal!

I learned more practical natural history from Hairy and his like than ever I learned at school. Such 'characters', highly skilled at their craft, were dying relics of the genuine countrymen that had been forced to adopt an urban lifestyle a couple of generations before. It would have been as impossible to tame his spirit and reduce his tenacity upon the lifestyle of his predecessors as it was to tame a lark. Hairy and his kind still brought a whiff of the countryside to the new urban 'estates' in spite of their minor eccentricities about what is mine or thine.

The transposed communities of that urban sprawl clung tenaciously to their rural roots. The squalid streets of Bloxwich merged into the equally impersonal streets of Walsall, which knitted in one amorphous mass right across the Black Country. Now that the population has been so thoroughly shuffled by the little man from the town hall, it is no more than a dreary conurbation. They insult it by the title West Midlands now, which has replaced part of South Staffordshire, Warwickshire and Worcestershire.

Nobody talked about going shopping in 'the street' in my young day. My mother met her friends in 'the village', enjoying village gossip with neighbours she knew personally. She would have been insulted if anyone suggested that she went shopping down 'the street'.

Bloxwich church was an ugly great red-brick barn of a building – but at least we thought of it as a *barn*, and not as an ugly great red factory, though the physical resemblance might have been equally compelling to outsiders who caused grave offence to the *villagers* if they said as much!

Moreover, the church and churchyard were encircled by a dry moat, with a vertical wall about 5 feet high surrounding the church property and a sloping bank rising to ground level on the village side. The moat was still known by the country name of 'ha-ha', and the sloping bank was to prevent livestock falling and getting stuck. They could easily climb out on the village side, though the vertical wall prevented them raiding flowers in the churchyard. The significance of our church ha-ha was that there would have been no need for it in a conventional town because there would have been no cattle or sheep or horses to stray on to church property. But a generation or so earlier Bloxwich had not been only a maze of bleak streets. The park had been a common, with grazing livestock where the bandstand now stands; the villagers really were 'commoners' with the rights to turn out stock on Elmore Green, and I was born in a house which once stood by the Pinfold (the traditional term for a pound for straying cattle).

We were all intensely proud of such pedigree, however far-fetched it must have seemed to strangers, because our instinctive rural roots were very deep. Curates like the Revd Davis, who scythed the church-yard for fodder for his horse, were taken as the norm. A city slicker who succeeded him regarded such husbandry as irrelevant because his one-track concern was his human flock. He was not so well received and one parishioner, who would have pretended to be out if she'd seen him coming in time, opened the door before discovering his identity. Flustered – and uncharacteristically discourteous – she blurted out, 'If it's religion you'm after, we're suited,' whereupon she shut the door.

My Old Man liked him no better – but was ostensibly more polite. He was driving his bull-nosed Morris down a country lane when the curate on his bike did an unsignalled U-turn immediately in front of him. Ancient Morrises were not famous for their brakes, so the Old Man trod on everything and 'scotched up', as we called it (from the days when waggoners put wedges under their wheels before descending a steep hill). He just missed the joy-riding cleric but, instead of letting forth a torrent of abuse as I might have done, he solemnly raised his hat and in the sweetest tone, 'Good morning, sir. I'm sorry to have to tell you, but you are exactly what you look.' My father said to me 'Good manners cost nothing, my lad.' We were half-way down the road before the recipient caught up with the fact that he had not received a compliment.

The Old Man was quite good at such remarks. I was with him when he had to 'scotch up' very suddenly, this time to avoid a kid who ran into the road. The chap behind was less alert and thumped us in the rear, so the Old Man got out to survey the damage, which was minimal, for ancient cars were tough and solid. 'Good morning, sir,' he said, raising his hat. 'And how do you stop, when I'm not here?' It was the perfect put-down.

Pat Collins, who owned travelling fairs which toured the whole county and called at intervals at his home in the village for refurbishment, overhaul or winter storage, was, in common with most of the Old Man's patients, esteemed as a friend of the family. He was already an old man when I knew him and he really had been through the whole gamut of change from rural roots to speculative prosperity. He had come to Staffordshire at the tail end of the last century as a raw young Irishman, determined to make his way among the travelling folk of fairs and circuses – and he certainly succeeded. He had a large house in the village, with a field he used all winter for storing roundabouts and steam boats, side shows and animal cages. It was cleared in July because, in August Bank Holiday week, 'The Greatest Show on Earth' – or one of them! – enlivened the village which flocked to the field behind Pat's house. This was known as Bloxwich Wakes.

Pat always asked the Old Man if 'the lad' was coming to the Wakes – and would have been mortally offended if the answer had been 'No'. I was invited to take my friends and to report at the house. Our host was always dressed in a frock coat, striped trousers and black hat, and he dyed his moustache and hair black until he was well into his eighties 'because a Showman must never look old', he said. He took us on to the fairground, where there was never any doubt that he was monarch of all he surveyed. From a lonely Irish lad, who had literally had to fight for a pitch at his first fair, he became mayor of Walsall, and a Liberal Member of Parliament for a short while. He always took us on a tour of his attractions, stopping at each in turn and holding up his hand.

The chair-o-planes, giant steam boats or dodgem cars stopped obediently. 'These are my young friends,' he told the man in charge. 'Give them a good ride.' Whereupon we got (for nothing!) a ride several times longer than normal, so we, in turn, were followed by a horde of other village brats (who were not Pat's 'friends'). They had to pay the normal rate for a ride, but they got better value for their money.

What I loved best about Pat's menage were invitations out of season. He always kept a good Alsatian bitch or two and, most years, he fostered one or two lion cubs on them, rearing them in the conservatory at the side of the house. As a great treat, I was invited to the house when the cubs were about as big as their foster dams, and allowed to spend a few hours playing with them. They were, of course, perfectly tame and fixated on dogs and humans, but the young naturalist in me found the experience very thrilling. Next Wakes Week I would see them in miserable cages about as big as hay wagons, boldly billed as 'forest-bred lions'. A significant sidelight on our modern 'multi-racial society', is that there had been no waves of immigration, in those days, and many of my friends had never even seen a black man. One year Pat had a lion tamer who had obviously originated in the same area as his lions and our local villagers turned out to stand and stare. The climax to his act was to put his head in a 'forest-bred' lion's mouth, which obviously didn't relish the experience and growled and snarled so fiercely that we were convinced that he really would bite off his trainer's head at the next performance. We should have known better, of course, because I recognized the 'forest-bred' lion as one of the sweetest-natured cubs I had played with the previous winter. But such is youthful gullibility that I fell for the ploy, going to encore after encore in the vain hope of seeing *real* drama when an obliging lion bit off the trainer's head.

Exotic as such experiences may have been, it was not slick showbiz but real country and real wildlife which had me instinctively enthralled – and so it is today. I have enjoyed the best part of a lifetime creating and managing a wildlife reserve where I am determined I will leave my bit of Britain better than I found it. Yet, strangely enough, it is not only such labours of love which leave the sweetest taste, but tiny incidents, insignificant in themselves, which are symbolic of ideals which dig deeper.

Peter was a case in point. We met as a result of a series of children's programmes I had been presenting for Dilys Breese, the distinguished natural history producer. We ran a competition to discover which children could identify the highest number of bird songs and call notes and other wildlife sounds we had recorded on tape. There were the usual book and record-token prizes, but the winner was to come for a day in my reserve where Dilys promised to make a programme in which he or she could record his impressions. It was a brilliant success.

The winner was Peter. He was an extremely articulate twelve-year-old, with his own tape recorder, to take home his own reactions, while

we recorded ours. He was at school at the Royal College for the Blind –
and he had been denied the faintest glimmer of God's daylight since
he was twelve months old. We got on fine.

I had a delightful old female roe deer at the time, who was free in
the wood but came to my study daily at coffee time. She would sell
her soul for chocolate digestive biscuits, so we started by introducing
Peter to her. He fed her with biscuit and ran his sensitive hands over
her, describing in detail to me the discoveries he made. I remember
the pleasure he got from fondling her sleek coat – and her surprising
confidence while being touched by a potentially menacing stranger.
But most of all I remember Peter's utter amazement at the length
and delicacy of her front legs. It was quite beyond him to imagine
how such apparently fragile limbs could propel their owner, at break-
neck speed, through the fallen logs and branches she must meet
every day in the dense cover of the wood. The observation, in retrospect, was blindingly obvious – yet I had *seen* her, with keen and
supposedly observant eyes – and the miracle had never even dawned
on me.

A young heron, fully fledged and ready to go, had fallen out of the
nest that morning, so I caught it and held it for Peter's manual
examination. I kept a firm grasp of its bill, because my guest would
have neither warning nor defence if it decided to get stroppy, and
again his reactions were original and perceptive. As we wandered
round the wood he kept stopping, earphone to ear, as he made his
own recordings of the sounds he heard and our conversation about
them.

The climax came at the far end of Holly Covert, where the herons
breed. A pair of pied woodpeckers had hatched off a brood in a hole
above the ground. Young woodpeckers ready to fledge are insatiable
and extremely noisy. They literally scream and chatter for their food,
so I shepherded Dilys and the lad in that direction without disclosing
what I knew. When we were 50 or 60 yards from the tree, I stopped
and bade them listen, for I thought (!) I could hear young birds calling.

Peter clapped his earphone to his ear and adjusted his recorder.
'They're too far off,' he said. 'I can't hear what they are. Can we get
nearer?' I said I thought we could, and we halved the distance. 'I
thought they were young starlings,' he said. 'But they're not. I don't
recognize them.' A pause as he listened and fiddled with his apparatus.
'Could they be young woodpeckers?' he asked. 'I've never heard them,
but I know they are noisy.'

I gradually led him to the tree and he held his mike up, as high as he could reach, which was a foot or so below the nesting hole. He grew very excited.

'They sound only just above my mike,' he said. 'How high is the hole? Could you lift me to it? I'd love to explore it.'

I hoisted him up and, running a finger round the hole, he described what he felt, explaining the diameter and his wonderment that birds could bore such large holes through solid, unrelenting oak.

Then he suddenly froze. 'I can feel the movement of the young birds inside the hole!' he exclaimed. 'Will they hurt my finger?'

'I don't know,' I said. 'You've got nine more. Try it and see!'

Tentatively he inserted a finger and he was suddenly suffused by the thrill of making an original discovery, which most naturalists are lucky to experience but once in a lifetime. 'They're *sucking* my finger,' he said. 'I can feel them sucking it.'

Those of us who are lucky enough to be fully sighted are so pre-conditioned to the notion that woodpeckers have long, intensely sharp and pointed bills that the idea that they could suck anything is totally preposterous.

'Come out of the way,' I said. 'Let me feel for myself.' I heaved him down and inserted my own finger in the hole – and was dumbfounded to discover that his description was uncannily accurate. It did feel as if my finger was being sucked!

The explanation was simple. Woodpeckers have exceptionally long tongues, designed for probing down narrow tunnels in woodwork to extract the grubs and beetles on which they feed. When Peter and I inserted our fingers, the fledglings 'explored' their potential by caressing or massaging them with their tongues. A cow's teat, being manually milked, must experience a similar sucking sensation!

It was a vivid demonstration of the advantages of a completely open mind unclouded by my preconceived convictions about what to expect; the intensity of that lad's instinctive pleasure in really being at one with Nature should be a lesson to those who are allowing our shrinking countryside to be exploited for profit. I found it a humbling experience, too, to discover that a blind lad of twelve could teach me so much about the wildlife that shares our wood.

Such salutary lessons would be unnecessary if there were a few more teachers around like Mary Sheward. I made friends with her, as I did with Peter and many other delightful people, through my work on radio and TV. Mary was headmistress of the school at Enville, on the Worcestershire-Staffordshire border. It was just a state primary school, reputedly the lowest form of life among the pseudo-elite of the academic world. Everything was wrong, by modern permissive standards, because the pupils were instinctively polite and well disciplined, with a hierarchy as rigid as a wolf pack. Staff and visitors were treated with courtesy and respect. Vandalism in the catchment area was unknown and the children there positively enjoyed going to school. I should even have enjoyed such schooling myself.

I first heard about it on the rural writers' grapevine which relayed the message that the primary school at Enville was so successful that local doctors, lawyers and other professional people no longer sent their children to expensive prep schools but that they were prepared to move house to get into its catchment area. This local state school was now regarded as better than the best in private education. I called to investigate. Mary Sheward was the reason for the school's success and her secret was that she geared the whole of her curriculum to the environment. She was greener than green without being a crank. Everything from maths to English hinged on the values that are now the incentive driving vast numbers of townsfolk to seek sanity in the countryside.

Mary had the conventional 'nature table', and the kids were encouraged to find and identify the flowers and trees and insects round about, not as a chore but as something to enjoy, which could be exhibited on the nature table. Within sight of the school rooms, in the grounds of the local estate, there was a medium-sized heronry and the school made regular visits there to do an annual count of the nests with follow-up visits to monitor the progress of the young. There was a proprietorial air about it, for the children were encouraged to feel that they shared it with the landowner. When nests increased there was satisfaction, and worry when the numbers went down. Either way, there were discussions and visits from specialists on herons to explain the fluctuations.

That heronry was not limited to natural history observations. It also taught maths the easy way. A chart recorded the annual numbers, rising and falling with success and failure, so that simple graphs and charts really meant something, instead of being mere dull statistics. Mary used to ask the kids how far away they thought the nests were – and she got surprising answers from yards to miles. So they all walked across, solemnly counting their steps. The tallest did it in about 420 while the tiddlers clocked up 500. Then they pushed a wheel, which did a revolution per yard, which recorded 440, give or take a rev. or two. Then, to be perfectly sure, they borrowed a surveyor's chain and measured the distance accurately. By the time they had done, a quarter of a mile really meant something to those children. They had measured it in so many ways, they could really visualize it!

Then Mary let them play with a stopwatch, which is a delight to all curious kids of that age group. They clicked it when a heron rose in the air from the nest and clicked it again when it flew directly over the school. The elapsed time was how long it took to fly a quarter of a mile, from which the arithmetic to calculate how fast it flew was a pleasure instead of a chore.

She discovered that the children were not very good at geography; maps didn't really mean anything to them. So she wrote to a shipping company, which gave her permission to take a party of her kids over a boat when it came into port. The captain was so impressed by their searching questions and enthusiasm that he persuaded some of his crew to 'adopt' a child or two and write to them, encouraging them to write back. Each time he berthed the captain brought a present back: a crocodile skin or a piece of crockery or a native weapon, which were displayed on the school notice board, along with a mark on a map to show where they had come from. When the ship was eventually broken up, the school was presented with the ship's bell. Geography meant something.

My experience as a broadcaster has taught me that it is relatively easy to get manually skilled people to talk freely and articulately about their physical achievements which they can visualize. Chainsmiths and shepherds, dry-stone wallers and stockmen are riveting when discussing the techniques they have mastered. But ask them about the satisfaction they reap from such work, or what memories they hope to leave behind, and their replies are likely to be more hesitant and tentative.

Mary found the same thing when trying to encourage her kids to talk about abstract subjects, so she used to take the tiddlers up on to Enville Common and allow them to play in and around an enormous hollow oak tree, which they loved. In due course she asked them to imagine what that oak had seen in olden times. The pragmatic ones might say that that was the tree where Mr Fox had always been able to escape when hounds were at his brush. He was slim enough to dive in where big hounds could not follow. The visionary ones said that it was where Robin Hood met Maid Marian or where Shakespeare wrote his sonnets. The range of replies was infinite – the respondents learned, subconsciously, what abstract thinking means.

Mary Sheward sensed the impending nostalgia of our insecure society for simple, solid, wholesome, ungimmicky country values. She was a generation before her time and, when she retired, they shut down her school because they thought it was old hat. We pay for such decisions with tax from our own hard-earned income – so we deserve what we are prepared to put up with!

THREE

The Big House

No single factor has contributed more to the erosion of the countryside and the security and traditions of countrymen than the decline of great estates. 'The Big House' and 'the Family' who lived there have been at the heart of every English village for centuries. Green-eyed trendies, who turn every news bulletin into a party political broadcast, scoff at such institutions as being paternalistic and patronizing. They whinge that no man should be allowed to own so much. 'The countryside belongs to the people,' they cry, 'not to the privileged few.' But as a naturalist I know that there is a rigid peck order in most successful species, and that it provides a strict code of conduct.

I live now in an area of Staffordshire which, until recently, comprised a number of adjacent great estates where the boundary of one merged with the next, extending about 20 miles across. It had remained entire for countless generations. As a result neighbouring landowners, whose ancestors treasured the same land before them, resisted the blandishments of speculative developers because they preferred to leave 'their' patch of countryside as good as, or better than, their forebears found it. Easy money meant less to them than their philosophy. We owe to them the glorious, random patchwork of spinneys and woods and the jig-saw of little fields which make the English countryside more peaceful and beautiful than any foreign lands.

My Old Man's practice survived among the dereliction of the industrial Black Country, but there were still lanes and farms along its boundaries, so that a number of farmers also joined our circle of friends. As a result of their hospitality, I had more broad acres to roam than if we'd owned a stately home.

There was but one stately home in the practice at Hilton. It belonged to the Vernon family who claimed to have come over with William the Conqueror. Three generations of the Vernons, known locally as the Old Squire, the Squire and the Young Squire, had a dramatic effect on my life. This was partly because each in turn allowed me the freedom of his land, but also because I had the chilling experience of observing, at first hand, the disintegration of the Hilton estate from 6000 acres to nothing over the same three generations which were spanned from my own grandfather to me.

My introduction to the Old Squire was accidental. Doctors not only knew their patients personally in those days, but they also visited them when they were sick instead of sending them to hospital or demanding attendance amongst the coughs and sneezes at the health centre. When I was on holiday from prep school I used to accompany the Old Man on his rounds, and he left me sitting in the car outside the Big House while he visited the Old Squire's wife indoors. The car was parked under the huge portico built outside the front door so that visitors could alight from their carriages and ascend an impressive flight of steps to the house without getting wet.

Grass grew through the gravelled drive, the lawn was covered with moss and there were more weeds than flowers in the garden. The whole place looked seedy and shabby because, by the end of the First World War, parasitic taxation was eating into the entrails of most of such great estates. Shabbiness meant nothing to me as a kid of ten or eleven, however, because the whole area which was 'home' could hardly be called picturesque. The Old Squire still owned six thousand or so acres, but he was already becoming impoverished and had been forced to sack gardeners and keepers and folk who worked in the house in order to remain solvent. It was perhaps significant that his first priority was to retain his estate intact instead of flogging his land to retain a life of personal luxury.

The garden of the Big House was bounded by steel railings, set close enough to exclude rabbits, and there was parkland outside this fence, dotted with small copses and plantations, provided by previous generations as cover for pheasants. The copses had not been laid out in any boring geometric pattern, as draughtsmen in modern planning offices might arrange them. Some had been planted on the summit of high ground, so that pheasants, driven from one, would fly high, over guns waiting below, to the refuge on the next high ground. Prolonged observation established the 'natural' flight lines chosen by generation after generation of birds. Coverts were then shifted or modified, so that with the advantage of prevailing winds and compromise between natural flight line and location of their objective, birds were forced to fly in a curve or arc, which obviously made it more difficult to shoot them. The squires and their guests were more interested in their prowess at hitting difficult or 'sporting' birds than in numbers in the bag at the end of the day. Other coverts and individual specimen trees had been deliberately sited to give spectacular or tranquil views from the house or to those who walked in the grounds for pleasure.

Young philistine that I was, I was no more interested in the aesthetic qualities of the estate than I was in the glaring symptoms of an early decline. What took my eye were literally scores of rabbits grazing on the impoverished turf in the park and hopping around in the wilderness of *ponticum* rhododendrons. I thought of Mick, my lemon-eyed mongrel, at home and of the ferret in her hutch in the garden and, as countless others must have done, I day-dreamed of the delight I would feel if ever I had the luck to own an estate of my own.

That fantasy was the moment the Old Man chose to emerge from the great front door and come down the steps with the Old Squire. I could hold my tongue no longer and asked if I could have a rabbit.

The sporting aspect of such estates has traditionally been one of their top priorities. In Norman times strict forest laws decreed precisely who could hunt what, defined by social status. Only the king could hunt beasts of the forest or fly a gyr falcon. Noblemen could fly a peregrine and hunt beasts of the chase; bishops and other hangers on were granted more privilege than their status warranted. Yeomen could hunt hares and fly goshawks while, at the bottom of the social peck order, parsons were allowed a sparrow-hawk!

Such human predation could have made no serious impact on the fauna of a well-wooded countryside for centuries until the first incursion of technology when bows and arrows and hawks were replaced by the invention of shotguns firing scatter shot. At a stroke, the necessity of stalking prey and shooting it, while motionless, exploded into the possibility of hitting flying game. The sheer numbers of quarry killed escalated beyond imagination and, as skills increased, it became desirable to lay out whole estates for the convenience of sportsmen – with the beauty of such varied countryside as the fringe benefit.

Landowners were naturally jealous of their privilege and the Old Squire was no exception. He had his estate festooned with warning notices announcing: 'Trespassers will be Spifflocated', and as few understood what the rite of spifflocation entailed, trespassers were few and far between.

A prep school lad boldly asking for the privilege of rabbiting was totally unheard of. Even the Old Squire's tenant farmers were allowed to catch rabbits only on their own farms when the game-shooting season was over. The law said that no agreement could prevent them killing the vermin that predated their crops – but they knew that the law was an ass because the Old Squire would not have renewed their lease if they had pushed their luck too far.

The obvious answer to cheeky youngsters who tried to muscle in on the act would have been to tell them to get lost, but the Old Squire took good manners and respect from others for granted and dispensed the same currency in return. Although I was not an invited guest, I was the son of his medical adviser, who was considered as such to be a friend of the family, which precluded the response of a curt rebuff. Eyeing me up and down, he came to the conclusion that I would pose no great threat to his rabbits – so he told me to bring some salt, the next time I came, and put it on their tails. I could have all I could catch. He was a generous man!

The result was that he introduced me to Mr Hannam, his head keeper, because protocol decreed that *nobody* could catch rabbits on the estate without his knowledge, if not approval. In many ways he wielded more power locally than his master, because tenants who were 'difficult' about conserving game might have their reputations smirched so that their tenancy was mysteriously terminated. Farm labourers who were 'difficult' were soon looking for a job elsewhere, and it was unwise for locals to complain too loud if a cherished pet cat did not turn up next morning, for Mr Hannam dispensed one-way tickets to terminate the travels of such unwanted strays.

Mr Hannam showed me his vermin pole with the greatest pride. A stout wooden rail nailed between two trees, was festooned with the decaying corpses of almost any species with canine teeth or a hooked bill, and any creatures keepers rate as 'vermin'. There were stoats and weasels and hedgehogs, hawks and owls, crows and jays and magpies – and there would have been badgers if the keepers had not long since exterminated all badgers on the estate. There weren't any foxes, because it was then regarded as a social crime to kill a fox except by hunting, and hounds were expected to 'find' one every time the hunt met on the estate. Subsequent experience suggested that the fugitive may have 'escaped' from Mr Hannam's sack on one side of a covert when hounds were thrown in on the other! Being a fox was a high-risk occupation in that part of the world. Cats, however, were the bane of his life and one end of his vermin pole was covered by cats' tails nailed to it. Ladies who objected were told that they should keep their mogs at home.

It was a rum kindergarten for a young naturalist whose instinct was to enjoy wildlife, not destroy it, but I learned a lot of tricks of an off-beat trade which are still a mystery to most of my more respectable friends.

Because so many of the Old Man's patients were also our family friends, I knew many miners who were great characters in their own right. Colliers, in those days, preferred poaching to picketing, so I would eavesdrop on the keepers' plans while ferreting rabbits by invitation, acting as a 'mole' to discover the tactics of the 'enemy'. On the way home I would call on my miner mates and tell them where the keepers would be that night. The reward for my duplicity was to accompany them catching rabbits in 'long nets' or with whippets with virtual immunity from detection because there was nobody patrolling our chosen beat. Rabbiting by invitation in the morning and poaching on the same estate at night might be regarded as an eccentric way of learning natural history – but it was certainly pragmatic.

The colliers, who enjoyed sport as keenly as their aristocratic – if unwilling – host, probably came of lineage as ancient and rural as the Old Squire himself. Instead of being swept away to towns and factories by the irresistible population migration of the Industrial Revolution, they had stayed put in the rural landscape of their ancestors and earned their living below the surface of the earth instead of as farm labourers on the land above.

The attitude to poaching of the big landowners of that era spells out the difference from modern times. Mass poaching, by gangs of the type of hoodlums that haunt football stadia today, was virtually unknown and the few cases brought to trial were rigorously stamped on. Thugs who raided rearing fields or release pens for the profit of large-scale sales were dealt with as the common thieves they were. The squires all presided in turn on the local bench and, although protocol demanded they stand down when the accused was alleged to have operated on their land, the JP who took their place well understood the principle of team loyalty among the beaks.

Poaching 'for the pot', however, was not regarded as a crime. Times were tough, families large and working countrywomen survived on a tight budget. A hard-pressed husband who poached a few rabbits for the stewpot or a pheasant for Sunday dinner would get a double helping of tongue pie from the beaks upon the bench, but he was secretly respected for looking after his family.

If it was a fair cop, his long nets or other equipment would be confiscated and he could consider himself lucky to get off with a small fine. Those who raided release pens or were otherwise involved in large-scale offences got what they deserved.

But poachers were not powerless. Sometimes a keeper grew disgruntled because his quarry was more cunning or fleeter of foot than he was. Such pillars of the law might not be above fabricating a little evidence, as sometimes happens even in our times. Poachers with a grievance had – and still have – an effective remedy. They waited till the keeper had the major part of next year's crop of birds incarcerated in a release pen, safely surrounded with wire netting high enough to keep the foxes out – or in. They would then dig out a litter of strong fox cubs around the middle of June, when they were self-supporting and about as big as large cats, and drop them inside the release pen. Panicking pheasants are totally irresistible to such predators, even when released inside the pen. By morning every pheasant would be dead at the jaws of a hunting fox. Keepers who left themselves vulnerable to such retribution had only themselves to blame. Not many tried it twice.

In those days the countryside itself was still veined by the rolling English lanes which had been left as haphazard trademarks by the original rolling English drunkard. When they had first been made, their course had simply followed the line of least physical resistance or the boundaries of the farms they skirted. Since nobody moved over them faster than a horse could trot, they had caused neither congestion nor accidents. When the coal pits came, powered by the great steam engines of the Industrial Revolution, this peaceful scene changed dramatically. First there was a constant procession of horses and carts along the now inadequate roadways and then canals were cut from Birmingham to Merseyside to get coal to the sea or to vast industrial towns. Reservoirs were constructed to 'top up' the canals, making good the water losses as boats were raised and lowered by chains of locks, which climbed or fell to keep pace with the changing contours of the countryside. Such transport facilities were still not enough, so railways were built to carry truckloads of coal further and faster than it could go on the sluggish canals. Worst of all, obscene pyramids of sterile clay towered above the pits as 'pit bonks' or 'tacky bonks' to advertise afar Man's inventive prowess at 'winning' black treasure from the belly of the earth.

An older generation than mine must have shuddered at the vandalism which exploited what should have been our heritage and the heritage of those that followed. The Old Squire himself must have writhed to see the land of his fathers ravished by technology and greed. Or perhaps he was practical enough to realize that taxation which robbed the rich and ruined the countryside would have bankrupted him totally if he had not received a small royalty on every ton of coal mined from below the surface of his land.

Health and safety inspectors were unheard of in those days and colliers were expected to be able to cope with almost any disaster which might befall. As it could easily be a matter of life or death to them, they took first aid very seriously and inter-colliery first aid competitions were held annually. To be a member of the winning team was a highly coveted honour. It was an ambition for which the Old Man had the very highest respect, because he took his own professional ability very seriously. He had a surgery – at our house, for there were no health centres in those days – every morning of the week but Sunday and every night but Saturday and Sunday. He practised till he was seventy-eight and every year till he retired attended his old hospital (the London) for a week's post-graduate course to keep himself 'up to date'. He claimed to be the oldest student there! The colliers had the highest admiration for such dedication, so every Thursday evening, when he finished surgery at eight o'clock, he motored 3 or 4 miles over to the Old Squire's pit, at Holly Bank, to instruct the pit's first-aid class.

The lanes he traversed were narrow and winding and, one night, a racing cyclist came, nose to wheel, full tilt towards him. The Old Man 'scotched up' to a standstill and honked his horn, but the oncoming cyclist couldn't stop, hit the car head on and sailed over the handlebars, over the bonnet and through the windscreen, to land in a heap on the passenger seat. It was before the days of splinter-proof glass and our old bull-nosed Morris had a screen of thick plate glass which cut the chap's face to ribbons.

The Old Man turned his uninvited passenger right way up and checked that there were no arteries severed. Then he got out and surveyed the damage to his car, which was minimal. The bike was a write-off, so he chucked it in the ditch. No formalities such as reporting the accident to the police ever crossed his mind. He simply climbed back into the car, told his gate-crashed passenger to sit tight, and he'd soon be all right, and continued on his way to the first-aid class. On arrival he apologized for being late but added that he would make up for the delay by giving a practical demonstration. He then proceeded to dress the wounds and stitch his patient together as neatly as a seamstress, giving a graphic running commentary during the whole of the unanaesthetized operation. It was a great success enjoyed by all – except, perhaps, the patient.

Regarding medicine as a calling, not a profitable chore, the Old Man prophesied that Nye Bevan's vaunted National Health Service would turn doctors from skilled professionals to sordid tradesmen. Despite his dedication to mastering the latest techniques, he was fascinated by the relics of rural folk medicine which still persisted in an industrial environment. When miners had an accident down the pit, for instance, they did not rush for antiseptics to dress the wound. They got their mates to piss on it, because urine is surprisingly sterile and washed the coal dust and grit away before it had time to cause infection. The Old Man discovered that country folk believe spiders' webs are ideal for staunching bleeding – though their antiseptic qualities in the pure air of isolated countryside would obviously have been better than in the dust-laden, polluted atmosphere round the Black Country where we lived.

If a new patient asked to be put on his list, the Old Man called at the house unannounced, expecting to be offered a cup of tea as a matter of course – and examined his surroundings closely while his hostess was getting it. If he couldn't see a spider's web, he passed her to his assistant. His theory was that any woman who sweeps away every spider's web is probably so prissy and house-proud that she will be a hypochondriac and cause more trouble than she is worth.

But his pet hates were drunks on Saturday nights who called him out to dress their wounds when they had been damaged in drunken brawls. He caused maximum discomfort while stitching them up and then stood over them while they drank a nauseous draught of his 'special physic', which would cool their blood. What he did not say was that it would also open their bowels and keep them glued to the closet for the next forty-eight hours, ensuring that they could not trouble him again during that weekend!

When the Old Squire died, death duties ravished the estate, forcing his son, the Squire, to sell off about two-thirds of his heritage, leaving him with about 2000 acres. He was a kind and dignified man, far less extravagant than his father, and the fragmentation of his lands was as traumatic for him as for many of his tenants, whose farms had to be sold over their heads, and his employees, who found themselves out of a job for the first time in their lives. By today's standards the price of land was catastrophically low. Good farms changed hands for £20 or £30 an acre – they would now fetch more than a hundred times as much. Cattle were knocked down for a tenner or less, sheep for a few shillings.

The Squire himself had never been employed. The army, the navy or the Church were permissible occupations for the sons of such families, but to take orders from lesser fry would have been considered socially unacceptable. Because it was 'not done' for the gentry to take any personal interest in 'trade' or commerce, many old estates were mismanaged by professional agents, who varied enormously in both integrity and competence. Whether it is preferable to provide benefits for the bent or to allow the blind to be led by the blind is a difficult choice.

Mr Hannam, as head keeper, survived because he was indestructible – but most of his staff of under keepers were made redundant with the exception of a couple of old stagers, who were prepared to stay on for a pittance. It was Hobson's choice, for nobody else would employ them.

The Squire extended his father's invitation to me to carry on rabbiting on the estate and I was often invited in for lunch. Those who equate riches with class might have been astonished to discover how frugally such people lived. I came to the conclusion that shepherd's pie was their staple diet! The whole house exuded an air of shabby gentility in the losing battle to keep as much of the estate as possible above the financial plimsoll line. Holidays were pie in the sky and the Squire's only recreation was the sport which his ancestors before him had enjoyed for countless generations.

In palmier days, previous Squires of Hilton had been famous for their racehorses, and Diomed, the winner of the first Derby, had been bred there. An oil painting of the horse, hanging in the hall, commemorated what the family felt was its only claim to fame. Solid oak post-and-rail fences behind the house still bore witness to the fact that such luxurious paddocks and five-star looseboxes had once been the home of equine aristocrats. Their only occupant, when I knew them, was a solitary hunter on which the Squire enjoyed a day's hunting most weeks in winter. The master of hounds would doubtless welcome such a major landowner, as an honorary member, and the grass in the paddocks was free, as were oats from the home farm, so that nobody could call this leisure pursuit an extravagance.

My father-in-law, more the Old Squire's vintage, also hunted with the South Staffs and Albrighton Hounds, but there were none of the luxuries of sending a horse to the meet in a horsebox while its status-symbol-seeking owner arrived in style in a Range Rover. Until the 1980s it was still accepted practice to ride (or 'hack') one's own horse anything up to 15 miles to a meet, hunt all day, and hack it home at night. The modern, effete, gin-and-Jag set would swoon at the thought.

The fact that the countryside was then still divided into little fields surrounded by well-laid hedges affected hunting style too. It was a competitive sport and real men rode straight. That is to say, they took a direct line across country in the same direction as the pack, and it was a matter of skill, pride and honour to jump any fence or other obstacle which appeared between the rider and the hounds he was following. Moreover, in the Old Squire's and the Squire's days, the old-fashioned rotation of crops was practised, and stubbles, after an autumn harvest, lay fallow all winter before being ploughed and seeded with spring corn. Nobody minded the hunt galloping *en masse* across old stubble, and huntsmen then took pride in knowing for themselves which crops would be damaged if they galloped across them. Good manners and rural courtesy decreed that guests, whether invited or following hounds, caused no offence by trampling the crops of their host. Today's farmers follow different cultivation methods and do not want hordes of horses galloping freely over their crops, so each hunt has a field master who leads his followers, like a bevvy of riding-school wenches, round headlands and lanes and verges where they will do minimal damage.

The Squire's other recreation was shooting. Mr Hannam and his geriatric beaters had long passed the age of 'presenting' driven birds to waiting guns, so the Squire and one or two guests 'pottered round', as they termed it, with a spaniel apiece to flush skulking birds from thick cover and hedge bottoms. It was an unglamorous form of 'rough' shooting, but it demanded intimate knowledge of the quarry's habits, the terrain it chose – and sensible, steady, working dogs. If each guest had a brace or brace and a half of birds to take home to his larder, everyone was satisfied. There was time and opportunity to see and enjoy all sorts of wildlife which never contributed to the total 'bag' at the end of the day. It was a far more civilized form of sport than the status-symbol circus act of modern greedy shooting syndicates which fork out fortunes – usually covered by business expense accounts – to compete with others like them for the 'honour' of shooting the greatest head of game. The vulgar winner may also pocket a 'sweepstake' of fivers, extorted from friends before the first drive.

Shooting was revolutionized as much by the physical needs of mechanized farming as it was by the financial constrictions of taxation which made adequate staffs of gamekeepers no longer a tolerable expense. In my childhood days, corn was cut in the field by a mechanical 'binder', a noisy, rattling contraption, with a jagged oscillating cutting bar protruding at one side like the knives on the axles of Queen Boadicea's chariot in my history book at school. There was a skeletal wheel rotating above the cutting bar which kept the standing corn erect and rigid while it was cut, and then guided it into the bowels of the machine. Here it was bound into bundles – from which the machine derived its name – and spat out on to the ground as sheaves on the opposite side to the cutter bar which had reaped them. The sheaves were then picked up by labourers and stood on end in small groups known as 'stooks', to be dried by wind and sun before being carted to the rickyard to be stacked in ricks till the threshing machine called.

Pulling the binder was hard work, demanding three huge carthorses, and persuading them to manoeuvre in small fields of 5 acres or less demanded a highly skilled wagoner. Among my happiest memories, as a lad of ten to twelve or so, was being perched on the back of the lead horse on a local farm at harvest time. My job was to guide it to turn sharp at the corners of the field to cut the next parallel swath. There was an immense sense of responsibility for a small boy perched so high, for the ground looked a mighty long way below! What is more, the bird's-eye view enabled rabbits to be spotted crouching in the corn long before they made a bolt for freedom and, although the jolting was hard on the backside, the discomfort was minimal compared to that endured by the labourers stooking the sheaves, whose forearms would be badly scratched by thistles and by the straw itself.

Tractors spelt the end of all that, for no small boys are needed on the bonnet as an aid to navigation. Worse still, tractors soon grew too big to manoeuvre in small fields, thus causing the modern scourge of grubbing out hedgerows, to make larger and larger fields, so that clumsy juggernauts can cavort in comfort. It is, of course, obvious that thick hedges form ideal nesting cover for birds and that, if you remove them, you lose the breeding habitat and concentrate surviving nests in less and less space – which makes them easier for predators to find. What is less obvious is that all sorts of wild creatures, from mice to muntjac deer and from hares to badgers and foxes, use hedges, ditches and verges as their natural channels of communication from one area of country to another.

Farmer-bashers blame the farmers for spoiling the countryside in this way, but the real culprit is the technological revolution which is as ruthless at forcing change upon us as the Industrial Revolution which preceded it. It is one reason for encouraging creative conservation by way of allowing natural regeneration in uneconomic areas and planting trees and cover to replace lost hedges wherever possible, not only by dedicated do-gooders but by everyone who values the future of the countryside.

While embryos of modern arable farming were still in the process of gestation, intensive livestock husbandry was changing rural ethics. The farmer who allowed me to ride lead horse at harvest also let me hang round the cowsheds at milking time. The sweet taste of fresh milk, at body heat, drawn straight from the udder into a glass is another cherished memory. However high the hygienists raise their hands in horror, I'm still crowing at over seventy-six, so it's taken a good while to kill me if it is as dangerous as they pretend!

Another memory of that cowshed of my youth is the smell. Good cattle, kept on sweet straw by skilled stockmen, have a wonderfully agreeable odour that is as much a part of real countryside as the song of larks or the sight of primroses in hedge banks or bluebell-bottomed woods. Even the piles of steamy muck outside the cowshed door smelled wholesome and pleasant, in total contrast to the foetid pong of modern slurry pits which collect the waste of beasts kept intensively in steel-and-concrete buildings. No small wonder that there is such deep nostalgia for organically grown vegetables, undefiled by the obscenities of intensive husbandry.

When the Squire died and the Young Squire inherited the remnants of his estate, the taxman dipped his groping fingers in the till again and death duties stole all but 600 acres or so. By then tenants were protected and times were very hard, so nobody wanted to buy farms that were let to tenants who couldn't be evicted. The result was that farms were sold so cheaply to sitting tenants that they more than recouped the purchase price by selling turf or hedgerow trees.

At least one farmer exploited a new technique of spraying the field with 'weed' killer to 'improve' the quality of the turf before selling it. This produced a total kill of the whole rich variety of wild flowers and herbs which become established in ancient meadows and which, by the modern standards of all but the most rabid, get-rich-quick, intensive arable men, would rightly be equated with sacrilege.

Once saleable 'pure' grass, fit for bowling greens or croquet lawns, had been achieved, a highly specialized mechanical turf cutter was used to take off extremely thin flat turves – which were worth precisely the same price per square foot as they would have been if cut 2 or $2\frac{1}{2}$ inches thick. The difference was that the uncut turf beneath recovered so quickly that another cut was possible a few months later, and a total of three cuts – each producing the total price paid for the land – were taken off the same fields in eighteen months.

Real farmers would say that selling turf is 'selling your fertility', and all leases in the olden days allowed the sale of crops growing on or harvested from the land, but not the land itself. Only spivs sell turf! Having more than recouped the purchase price of a cheaply bought farm by beggaring the land in this way, some deemed it smart to sell the land with vacant possession at many times the original purchase price and leave the mug who bought it to discover too late that he had bought a pup. In my day such deals were regarded as sharp practice. Now they are accepted as the norm of our 'enterprise culture'!

Although the Young Squire took hunting and shooting for granted, he was far more interested in natural history than any of his ancestors. When he moved into the Big House and discovered that I had been a visitor in the time of his father and grandfather, he invited me over to meet him. On arrival I was told that I would find him in the shrubbery, a long narrow slang of mature woodland which had long since risen above and shaded out most of the original shrubs. One side was bounded by the drive and the other by the moat, which did not surround the house but bordered two sides only.

I discovered the Young Squire, a very quiet, modest, rather slight man, standing motionless under a tree with a pair of binoculars. He was watching the spectacular courtship flight of a lesser spotted woodpecker, a smallish bird about the size of a starling, which is not common and spends so much time high in tree tops that it is rare to see one. I could count my previous sightings on the fingers of my hands.

We greeted each other briefly – and settled down to watch the woodpecker, which seemed to both of us to be more important. Only when the bird disappeared did we discover how much we had in common. Because of the difference in our age and status, I never knew the Old Squire well. He had simply been a distant figure, whose hospitality I had enjoyed and whom I had observed with interest, rather as his grandson and I enjoyed examining the habits of this lesser spotted woodpecker objectively. I was therefore fascinated to discover that the Young Squire himself had stood in awe of him. It had been the custom for the old boy to invite his grandson to the Big House for the last few days of his school holidays. They had little in common, and conversation was therefore stilted and superficial – until the last rites before he was dispatched back to boarding school when the ritual never varied.

'Goodbye my lad,' the old boy would say, pressing a 5 shilling piece into his grandson's palm. 'Say your prayers and keep your bowels open.'

And this was the last they would hear of each other till the next holiday.

But it was the Young Squire's instinctive love of wildlife which gave us so much in common. He tolerated teasels because they attracted charms of goldfinches, and nettles for butterflies, and he was far more tolerant of predators than any of his more sporting ancestors.

He phoned one evening with a simple message. 'Hannam has retired – and the badgers are back,' he said. 'Bring Jess over for a bite of supper and we will go badger watching.'

We needed no second bidding, for neither of us, at that time, had had the chance to watch badgers in the wild, although I had bottle-reared a cub, rescued from the diggers, and he had accepted us as members of his social group. It was a glorious summer evening and our host led us across the park to a bank crowned with huge *ponticum* rhododendrons, planted originally as pheasant cover. It would have been paradise out there, even if we had seen nothing but the view, because the pit bank of the colliery and all signs of industry were hidden by the woods and copses which surrounded the park.

Long before the light began to fade the silence was broken by scuffling and whickering in the undergrowth and, within seconds, three badger cubs, about three-parts grown, were rolling and chasing each other with mock ferocity out in the open. They were joined by the old sow and, as they grew more and more excited, their distinctive musky odour drifted over on the eddies of breeze till we relished them with all our five senses but taste and touch. I have watched wild badgers literally hundreds of times since then, because they feed within yards of our sitting-room window every night. But the thrill of that first sighting is as vivid now as it was half a century ago.

In retrospect, the Young Squire's reactions were far more significant for, he told us, one of his most treasured memories was of watching badgers at the same sett when he visited his grandfather during school holidays. Mr Hannam had not then arrived, so there were still a few places on the estate, not densely populated with game, where predators survived. New brooms sweep clean – and the new head keeper was no exception. Thereafter, my own experience tells me, badgers in search of new territory would have tried to recolonize the denuded habitat but each new immigrant would be issued with a one-way ticket and been snared or gin-trapped, dug out or poisoned before it had had time to settle.

So the sett we were watching had fallen in and been used only by rabbits for the whole of the head keeper's reign of half a century, give or take a few months. It is some yardstick of the havoc gamekeepers who are relying on 'wild' as opposed to intensively reared birds can wreak. (There is, of course, no need to exterminate all predators on a shoot now, because pheasants are hatched in multi-thousand-egg incubators and reared under electric or bottle-gas brooders. They are not liberated in woodland until old enough to fly into the trees high out of reach of foxes and badgers.) But what a marvellous thing that, within a few months of the retirement of a keeper who had destroyed every prospecting badger before it had had time to settle, the next wave of explorers should find and colonize a traditional ancient sett which had been denied to the species for the best part of fifty years.

The fact is that, if the right type of habitat is provided and security of tenure catered for, it is as practicable to persuade badgers and other species to settle happily as it is to tempt blue tits to use an artificial nest box. And with greater and greater human pressure on the rural environment, it becomes more and more necessary to 'manage' wildlife, persuading it to colonize country where incompatible intrusion can be kept at bay by whatever means are available.

It was the experience of seeing those first wild badgers happily installed in the sett their distant ancestors had constructed which fixed my determination to attract wild badgers to colonize setts I constructed in my own wildlife reserve.

Another great change the Young Squire witnessed on his estate was the introduction of 'chemical farming'. The advance of technology led to the discovery that arable output could be multiplied many-fold by the use of chemical pesticides, fungicides and herbicides and artificial manure (or 'bag muck'). When I sat on the lead horse of the binder, my farmer host was lucky to produce a ton of corn to the acre. Absentee landlords and their accountants, who control vast acreages of farmland today, would sack a farm manager who did not produce 3 or $3\frac{1}{2}$ tons to the acre. They do so by applying many chemicals that are so lethal and persistent that, in intensive arable areas, they have changed the whole population pattern of wildlife, slaughtering the innocent with what they regard as the guilty. The damage done by gamekeepers in the name of sport is as nothing compared to that wreaked by the agrochemical industry in the cause of greedy profit.

Once again, it is the farmers who catch the thick end of the stick, but what are their alternatives? Are they to abide by 'old-fashioned' methods and go out of business? Or are they to accept the wonders of modern technology just to keep solvent, while the multi-national moguls of the chemical industry grow fat?

As it is against developers who exploit the countryside, the most powerful defensive weapon is the weight of adverse public opinion. Unless enough voters make it plain to all political parties that conservation of the countryside and of wildlife are so important that votes will be lost by any party which does not take active steps to prevent the rich growing richer, at the expense of the countryside our heirs will inherit, the toughies will destroy what is left. Once it is made plain that decent people regard it as anti-social to mortgage the rural future, it will become a selling point to demonstrate that products and projects genuinely are 'environmentally friendly'.

The violent change which spelt the end of the Vernons' reign at Hilton was a direct result of two world wars. When the nation has a foreign dagger at its throat, no price is too high to pay for developing the weapons to beat the enemy. The First World War started with cavalry and finished with tanks, which put puny tractors and early motorcars in the shade. The great need of the Second World War was for aeroplanes to counter the threats of invasion or bombing by the Huns – and aeroplanes are no good without airfields where they can take off and land. Bulldozers therefore emerged as much more powerful, by comparison with tractors, as pre-historic monsters were to uncivilized Man. Overnight there were techniques available which could change the face of the countryside to make runways and hangers and all the ancillary bric-à-brac, from factories on farmland to munitions dumps hidden among the trees.

When war was over the mass-production of motorcars was one way of keeping wartime labour force and machine tools occupied but, as planes need airfields, cars need roads. These were also easy enough to build, given post-war civil engineering techniques, and the M6 motorway was constructed to run right through the Young Squire's estate – what was left of it. The Hilton Service Station virtually obliterated Mr Hannam's cottage and the motorway itself sliced off enough land to make the rest of the estate unviable.

It was the last straw and the Young Squire conceded defeat by what some regard as progress. He put the remnants of his family's land under the auctioneer's gavil, packed his bags and went away. For the first time in almost a thousand years there wasn't a Vernon at Hilton. It was the end of an era.

FOUR

TREADMILL

One snag about being the oldest or only son of a farmer or doctor is that it is likely to be taken for granted that you will assume the Old Man's mantle when he retires or dies. For as long as I could remember it had always been drilled into me that when I left school I should go to university and a hospital medical school so that I could join the practice as an assistant and end up as senior partner. Even I, a born rebel, never questioned it.

My stepmother, whom I couldn't stand the sight of, was a bit of a social climber and she wanted to tell her friends that 'her' son was at Oxford or Cambridge, so when the time came to escape from school I was shuffled off to Oxford. There was, of course, no difficulty about entry in those days. Anyone who matriculated at school would be accepted, at least in the less fashionable colleges, if his father stumped up the fee. Entrants were also as welcome if it were likely they would get a blue at rugger or rowing as if they were destined for academic distinction.

I went to Keble, which was stuffed with parsons' sons or budding parsons, and I turned up in the biology lab. for work next morning. There was a veritable giant of a man doing a dissection on the adjoining bench, who turned out to be the university heavyweight boxing champion. It was the third time he had taken first-year medicine without passing an exam, though whether this was because he was

keener on boxing gloves than scalpels or because he rarely appeared for
a lecture or demonstration, I never discovered. He had one eccentricity
which appealed to my naturalist's mind. On the back of his right hand
a dragon's head had been tattooed in almost stereoscopic technicolour.
Its fangs coincided with his knuckles when he clenched his fist. This
pre-historic monster's neck entwined his arm so that its body and legs
spanned his chest. The tattoo wound round his left arm, like a boa
constrictor, leaving the tip of the tail on his left knuckle. It was an
intricate feat of cosmetic surgery which doubtless gave defeated rivals
the excuse that they had been knocked out either by a dragon's head
or tail. The proud bearer of this macho scar denied that the operation
had been painful because he remembered nothing about it. His 'friends'
had caused it to be performed while he was drunk.

Although I stayed for two years, there was little else about Oxford
which appealed to me. The final straw was when I was required to
prepare to dissect a fellow mortal. Like most instinctive countrymen,
I have always been spooky about corpses. I refuse to 'view the corpse'
at funerals, making the excuse that I 'prefer to remember him as he
was', and I don't fancy going through churchyards at night. So when
I was shown a galvanized tank of what I think was formalin, with
several stiff, shaven bodies slurping around in it, and I was asked to
choose one for dissection, it put me off my grub. I decided that I
shouldn't like many of the patients in my father's practice when they
were well. Sod them when they were ill, and they would be quite
insufferable when they were deceased symbols of my failure to heal
them.

It was not easy to break the news to the Old Man that he had paid
my fees at Oxford for two years and given me a generous allowance
before I had made up my mind that I didn't wish to join him in his
practice, but he took it better than I had any right to expect.

'Right,' he said, 'if you don't want to *practise* as a doctor, stay on
the course and qualify before you pack it in. Then, having qualified as
a doctor, I will pay for you to stay on and take law. The medico-legal
profession is paid astronomic figures, quite out of context with its
worth, because of scarcity value.'

It was sound and practical advice – but I had no stomach for being
a lawyer either. The Old Man was less than amused and told me, in
no uncertain terms, that I'd better make up my mind what I was
going to do – and make the decision quickly. He had no intention of
supporting me in idle luxury much longer.

I happened to be passing through the teenage whizz-kid stage, racing motorbikes and sidecars instead of wrecking football stadia or throwing bricks at coppers, which seems to be the fashion with modern young tearaways. Since I couldn't afford to buy a good enough motorbike to win, I decided to opt for engineering, so that at least I would learn to tune my own engine.

The decision did nothing for the Old Man's temper. He said he was wasting no more money keeping me at Oxford to read *engineering*! If that was the height of my ambition, I could go to a London polytechnic and live in digs or to Birmingham University and live at home. He said he would make it bloody hard for me either way. I chose London because I could not bear the thought of being stabled with my stepmother for three whole years. School holidays had been more than enough for me!

London was hell. There were eighteen of us in the digs, which cost thirty bob (£1.50) a week, though the landlady was quite a character. Her husband worked as a clerk at the Inland Revenue and always wore a dark jacket and striped trousers. I remember the striped trousers very well because I used to have to deal with them quite often when he got paralytic drunk.

The landlady would buttonhole me and ask me to help get her husband to bed 'because he isn't very well tonight'. That meant he was spark out somewhere. When I found him I chucked him over my shoulder and deposited him on the double bed in a room beside the front door, where the landlady always slept to intercept unauthorized visitors or prevent her 'paying' guests doing a moonlight flit. The old boy was nothing but skin and bone, and little effort was needed to cart him round, so I used to take off his boots and tie and jacket and leave him right way up on the bed. I remarked one night, when he was particularly deeply unconscious, that he really did seem very poorly.

'Yes, Mr Drabble, he is,' she said. 'He isn't very strong, you know, so I don't take a penny of his wages from the tax office. He won't live very long. I *do* like to feel he's *enjoying* himself, so I leave him all he earns to spend. I do my part by running this boarding house – and I put any profit I make into an insurance on him.'

I often wondered if Hitler dropped a bomb on him before he croaked and did the old girl out of the 'death divi'.

The cook in those digs was over eighty. She cooked for eighteen of us for a wage of 10 shillings (50p) a week and her keep. Not surprisingly, she was not in love with mankind and she was utterly determined not to leave a penny of her stipend to anybody. So every Saturday night she went on the binge and blew her wages. About eleven o'clock one or other landlord from the locals would ring up and ask for somebody to be sent round to 'fetch your cook, who isn't very well!' We were far gentler with her than with the old man, but her malady was just the same.

I hated every day I was in London, which I found a most uncivilized place, utterly different from the urbanized Black Country where I grew up. Chaps at home were still real countrymen at heart; Londoners, I found, were slick, superficial Cockneys. They may have been perfect fodder for our present 'enterprise culture', but it was with the greatest relief that I wiped my feet of the place when the time came to launch myself into self-sufficiency.

Times in the 1930s really were hard. Jobs were difficult to come by and nobody with any sense strained to extract the last penny of wages. Security was then in lethally short supply – as people are beginning to realize it is now. 'A job for life' – at *any* wage – was far more important than 'big money today and God knows what tomorrow'. The dole was 'charity', and respectable folk despised it.

Apart from having completed an engineering course at a polytechnic, I had nothing to offer an employer. My desperate need was some practical experience. My hasty decision to do engineering in order to tune my own motorbike had cost me a life sentence. I spent the next quarter of a century mewed up in factories. Breaking into the first one with no real qualifications was the difficulty because, in those days, factory managers were expected to know enough about the job to show their men how to do it if the need arose but I experienced, for the first time, the inestimable value of the Old Boy Network.

The Old Man knew the manager of Sankeys, of Bilston, socially, so, much against his will, he asked him if he could give his lad a bit of practical experience before he set out to get a 'proper' job. The manager promised an introduction to *Mr* Hall, his foreman of the toolroom. It was made crystal clear to me that, once there, I should be totally answerable to *Mister* Hall, who was accustomed to hiring and firing his own staff and might resent having me wished upon him by the boss. If I didn't suit him, he would sack me. There would be no appeal.

It was a repeat performance of *Mr* Hannam and the Squire. The Squire was titular landowner, but it was *Mister* Hannam who carried the clout and made the decisions about running the sporting side of the estate, and who often had the say on which tenants and labourers survived and which didn't.

Mr Hall bristled when the boss introduced me. I don't think he ever discovered my name because he always called me 'Son', as he did all the other chaps in the toolroom. 'Son, do this or do that,' he would bark and there was no way of deciding whom he was talking to except by working out whom he was glaring at.

He told me he would pay me 45 shillings (£2.25) a week, and that they started at 8 am and finished at 6 pm except on Saturday, when they finished at 12 noon. The factory buzzer blew at *one* minute to eight and continued blowing for *one* minute. When it stopped, the gate was slammed and there was no way of clocking in after this. Those who were late were not reprimanded or docked ten minutes' pay, as they would be in these effete times. They were sent home for half a day. This was particularly onerous for me because the police had caught me driving a friend's car down Battersea High Street at 58 miles an hour during my last term at London. We were getting back to the digs, after tennis, to change for a dance, so there was no question of being drunk. I had just been in a hurry. But Cockney stipendiary beaks are narrow-minded little men and I had my licence suspended for four months. During my first winter at Sankey's, therefore, I had to travel to work on a pushbike. It was uphill both ways, the wind was always against me and it was usually raining, so Mr Hall had the pleasure of sending me home for half a day occasionally when I failed to beat the buzzer, and I didn't bother to come back for the afternoon. If I did that twice in a week, he told me to stay away the whole of the next week – for him!

It probably helped me with the chaps in the shop who realized he was picking on me and giving me the dirtiest and most boring jobs to try to break my spirit and make me pack it in of my own accord. Everyone was very sympathetic and helped me all they could – and I bought a Stafford bull terrier pup off one of them to celebrate my first week's wages.

I had a lot in common with the chaps in the toolroom because, like the descendants of so many other countrymen who had drifted in from the surrounding countryside a couple of generations earlier, they all seemed to have some rural hobby which monopolized their spare time. They competed in classes to grow giant onions or parsnips in tubes of fertile soil 4 feet deep. There were lots of members of 'the Fancy' too: not one particular 'fancy' but rabbit fanciers, who bred all sorts of exotic varieties, and canary fanciers, who entered their birds for singing contests. One man's life ambition was to produce the world's first pink mouse!

They had an extraordinarily basic, rustic sense of humour with a passion for practical jokes. Strutt, who wrote the classic *Sports and*

Pastimes of the People of England, published in 1805, describes 'the Grinning Match', which was 'performed by two or more persons endeavouring to exceed each other in the distortion of their features, every one of them having his head thrust through a horse's collar'. Strutt would have been at home in Sankey's toolroom.

I could just imagine my new-found mates entering such competitions with enormous zest, because nothing pleased them more than painting a mate's bike, in stripes, like a zebra or hoisting it to the top of the works crane a few seconds before power was cut off at Saturday lunchtime, leaving it dangling irretrievably aloft till Monday morning.

But the favourite jape took place occasionally in the men's lavatory at nine o'clock on Monday morning. There was a long line of twenty or thirty seats, each in a normal cubicle but, instead of having a pedestal for each seat, there was a deep glazed trough, formed from a half-pipe, which went the length of the whole building. This trough did not require a chain and flush for each cubicle. There was, instead, a large tank at one end which, when the valve was released, sent a surge of water along the whole trough, swilling the lot in one wave along the pipe to the far end of the cubicles.

There was a breakfast break of ten minutes at 9 am, which started a general rush for the loos, where everyone sat with the morning paper, picking his winners for the day. One of the labourers was an unofficial bookie's runner and he collected the slips at ten past nine and took them to the bookie.

The ritual Big Joke was perpetrated by one of the apprentices, who sneaked off a few minutes before nine and occupied the end seat, below the main flushing tank. About five past nine, when everyone was engrossed in picking his winners, the apprentice scrumpled up a large bundle of paper, as big as a football, floated in on the trough, put a match to it – and pulled the chain. The incandescent paper floated silently along beneath one punter after another, all down the line, producing more ribald mirth than the ugliest yokel ever to leer through a horse's collar.

Being dished out with all the dirty jobs by Mr Hall was a bonus in disguise. Knowing, from experience at the sharp end, just what it is like to be *made* to do something unpleasant and often very uncomfortable, with no chance of answering back without retribution, is wonderful experience when the time eventually comes to get in the saddle oneself. It cuts down arrogance to be able to visualize what the victim will think – if he doesn't put it into words. And it rings alarm bells, when one is tempted to pussyfoot, if personal experience dictates that the victim will think you are a wimp if you don't force the point.

Even Mr Hall accepted me in the end and he gave me experience on lathes and millers, shapers and precision drilling machines. I did hour after blistering hour of hand filing, all to high-grade toolroom standards of accuracy. When I left I understood what was reasonable and what was unreasonable to ask a man to do and could tell him to 'come out of the way while I show you' when he didn't come up to scratch or tried pulling wool over my eyes.

But my practical education would not have been complete without Fred. He was the shop steward and he taught me all the fiddles. If Fred couldn't break the system, it was unbreakable, and what I learned from him was of more use in my later career than anything I learned from academic lecturers.

When I was leaving, he wished me luck, saying that if ever I became a manager I'd be as big a bastard as all the rest. I thanked him prettily and told him not to apply for a job where I was the gaffer, because shop stewards like Fred wouldn't last for long. We parted with mutual respect and often met up for a pint.

Forty-five bob a week wasn't enough to get married on even in those days – but I had got engaged to Jess, whom I'd known all my life, when I came down from London. Her family were patients of the Old Man and I'd often gone to her house for children's parties – which I hated! – since I was about five.

Out of the blue, Robins, my sidecar passenger, a parson's son who had been at school with me, asked me to keep a specific date free a couple of months ahead. He said he was getting married and would like me to be his best man. I wasn't particularly interested in his life outside my racing sidecar and didn't even know he'd got a girl. He didn't seem the type but, to be polite, I asked him where he was going to live.

'Tanganyika,' he told me. He was going as assistant engineer on a sisal plantation.

The kernel in the nut was that he must be leaving his job in England, which was at Salters, the spring balance makers, in West Bromwich, so I asked him who had got it.

'Nobody, yet,' he replied. 'I haven't given my notice in.'

I asked him to put in a good word for me, as the job *must* be better paid than mine. He said it would do no good because the boss would be peeved about him leaving. But he told me he would give in his notice next Friday night.

On Saturday morning I went to reception in Salters' office and asked to see the managing director. A little man in a dirty mac appeared and asked me what I wanted.

'I want to see the managing director,' I replied, thinking this must be the assistant foreman.

'*I* am the managing director. What do you want?' he said.

'I want Mr Robins's job,' I answered.

This obviously took him aback, because he said that Robins had only given in his notice the night before so how did I know? Anyway, the place to apply for jobs was in the labour office downstairs. However, his curiosity got the better of him and he asked where I worked and what I did. We parted quite civilly and he said he would see what he could do and, if I didn't hear from him in the meantime, to get in touch in six weeks.

Hearing no more, I turned up again in six weeks to the day and demanded to see the managing director. The receptionist had obviously got a rocket for fetching the top brass to an unannounced visitor, so she asked if I had an appointment. I said I had.

The little man appeared again and gave no sign of recognition. He had obviously forgotten all about me but enquired if I had an appointment.

I told him I had and reminded him that he himself had asked me to get in touch in six weeks if I heard no more. So here I was. Six weeks were up today.

This obviously confused him, so he passed the buck by taking me to see his eldest son, who was works manager and wanted an assistant.

The poor son knew nothing about it and stalled for time by asking me, in great detail, where I was working and what I did. When the conversation dried up, he asked what salary I was looking for – if he did set me on.

I said I'd go for nothing for a month and that he could then pay me what he found I was worth.

This threw him completely – and he stuttered that that was not the way he was used to doing business. So he set me on for £3 a week – which was 15 shillings (75p) more than I was getting at Sankeys. After a few weeks I got a rise to £4 a week and a flat in the works, for which I was to be deducted 10 shillings (50p) a week. Jess and I got married.

I stayed at Salters for the next twenty-three years, doing the last seven on the board of directors, and I thoroughly enjoyed it while I was climbing the ladder. Once on the board, with nowhere further to go, I found it pretty boring.

Promotion was a bit like taking pennies off the baby. It was an old family firm, the last Salters being godparents to the family then in the saddle, to whom they had left it. When each generation of owners' sons came into the business, they were ritually 'put through the works'. That is to say, they spent six weeks in each main production department and six in the sales and administrative offices, by which time they were supposed to know precisely what everyone did. The fact was, of course, that they learned only what their employees wished them to learn. Everyone knew when a gaffer's son was in the department and took jolly good care that he saw nothing they did not want him to see. No fiddles or malpractices took place till the paternalistic intruder had moved on again.

It suited my book perfectly because I soon discovered that the boss men simply did not understand the psychology of the shop floor. They were totally out of tune with their workers, whom they described as 'very decent little men', because they had never mingled on equal terms. Having been brought up with the wide spectrum of my Old Man's patients, I was totally immune to 'class'. I didn't give a damn whether people I met were dukes or dustmen, because they were all alike to me – and they still are. I look them all in the eye, as equals, and admit to myself that most of them are better men than I am, so that we treat each other with mutual respect whatever nominal strata of society we come from.

My flat in the works was the top storey over a dentist and a shop in the high street, opposite the main works entrance. At the time we had Grip, the Stafford bull terrier I had bought as a pup off the chap at Sankeys with my first week's wages, and we soon learned the draw-backs of keeping a dog in town and having to climb down two flights of stairs every time he wanted to go out. Jess used to take him for a walk every afternoon in the local park, where she became very unpopular because he was a devil for chasing hares – which he never caught! The park keepers threatened to 'do' her for poaching. Grip had his compensations, though – he was a marvellous ratter. I managed to keep a few ferrets in an old, condemned cottage, which had been engulfed when the works had been extended a few years earlier, and Grip and I would go ratting every Sunday, while Jess was cooking lunch. We reckoned we did far more good to society than the local vicar!

Although it was a sordid, urban area, with back-to-back houses, in endless dreary, red-brick rows, the folk who lived in them were far more rurally than urban orientated. Each pub had its own close-knit clientele. There were gardeners' pubs, frequented by specialists in outsize specimens, and pubs where the whippet-men, bull terrier-men or pigeon-racers congregated. Offbeat sports such as breeding and flying tumbler pigeons, which executed so many back somersaults that the best birds sometimes spun out of control till they crashed to death on the ground below, were yet more tests of the stockman's skill.

The beerhouses were filled with fellow enthusiasts for practical hobbies and the common factor of all such diverse interests was a consuming pride in stockmanship or skill. The Old Cross Guns at Cradley Heath, for instance, was the hub of the chain and anchor trade, which made the district famous wherever ships were sailed. Joe Mallen, the landlord, was a master chainsmith who had his own gang of strikers and was personally responsible for the size of steel bar needed to forge such works of art as vast anchor chains for ocean-going liners and for the skill his gang needed to hammer the white-hot metal to its final shape. Designers in a drawing office meant nothing to him and when I called he often pulled a grubby scrap of paper from his pocket showing the final shape required and asked how I would set about it. Not surprisingly, I hadn't a clue. It would probably have taken him aback if I had. So he'd dip a horny finger in his pint pot and trace out on the pub table the secrets of his trade. Such skills and the quality of his bull terrier were his greatest pride in life.

Passing the pub in working hours one day, I dropped in for a pint and was surprised to find Joe, not in working clothes, but hunched morosely over the bar. His wife, Lil, an outgoing dynamo of irrepressible energy, ran the pub while he was at work, and when I asked what 'the boss' was doing in the bar mid-morning, she told me to ask him myself, as he hadn't been to work for a week.

Bit by bit the truth seeped out. 'They' had engaged management consultants at the works, who said the chain links cost more than they should because master smiths, like Joe, specified more material than was needed – and top-class steel was expensive. Bars of smaller cross-section were ordered and Joe told to make a sample link from that. He refused, saying that the size the boffins wanted would not stand the rigorous safety test applied by Lloyd's Proving House. The managing director insisted that the designers' specification was tried – giving the firm assurance that Joe and his gang would not be blamed if the link they forged failed when tested. Finally, under protest and pressure, a link was made but, as Joe had predicted, it failed to pass the test.

Tears poured down his cheeks as he recounted this personal tragedy. It was very moving to see this huge, beer-swigging hulk of a man bitterly ashamed because, for the first time in his working life, a link he and his gang had forged with loving skill 'disgraced' him when it was tested. Vainly I pointed out that smart-arse industrial consultants are the parasites of a get-rich-quick society, rotting the guts of trades where skill is being replaced by slick technology. Nothing I could say soothed his injured pride. He hadn't been to work since 'his' link failed, nor did he go till the managing director called personally at the pub to assure him, in front of his mates and customers, that he blamed the design consultant and there was no slur on either the smith himself or his skilled gang. Come back the Bad Old Days.

It is not surprising that such simple, sentimental souls retained their basic, rustic sense of humour. Joe used to recount, with mock tragedy, how poor he used to be and how hard the old times were.

'Why, Phil,' he'd say, 'when we got wed we *were* very poor. As we was walking up the aisle, I sez, "How much money have you got, Our Lil?" "Half-a-crown, Joe," she replied. "Chuck it away then," I said. "Let's start level"' [which he pronounced 'leveel' in his rich Black Country brogue].

Anyone complaining of being off the hooks got the benefit of his practical advice. 'Only the good die young,' he'd say. 'So be as bad as thee con'st,' adding after a suitable pause, 'then you'll live to be a hundred – and I shall come to your funeral!'

Old Sam Careless was usually propping up the bar at the Old Cross Guns, wearing a blue serge suit, with a gold watch-chain looping across his ample belly, a flashing diamond ring on his finger and a glamorous blonde in a fur coat swigging gin by his side. Sam had had a horse and cart before the war, delivering coal, but he had obviously made a lot of brass since then, though one didn't ask how. When I enquired if he'd had his holidays one glorious summer day, he was obviously taken aback. 'Holidays?' he said. 'Holidays? I ain't done no work for fifteen years. But I've done a hell of a lot of *schemin'*.'

Knowing such characters intimately, on level terms, was an incalculable advantage to me at Salters because it meant, when I was invited to join the board, that I was constantly asked my opinion about how possible policy decisions would be received. I was bilingual enough to speak the language of the shop floor and predict reactions to proposed change and yet convey it to fellow directors who had never had a blister on their hands.

The managing director of Salters was chairman of the Chamber of Commerce and Industry, a pretty big wheel among Midland industrial tycoons. He was invited to join the management board of the Midland Engineering Employers' Federation, which was an honorary, part-time appointment. He declined because it entailed an intimate knowledge of shop-floor politics, which were quite out of his sphere. He offered me as an alternative, which took the federation aback, because the object of their exercise had been to recruit a big name who would swim with the tide, not some unknown nonentity whose reactions to their wishes might be unpredictable.

I accepted with pleasure and was summoned to lunch in a private room in the city of Brum's most prestigious hostelry. I arrived on time but was stood up and left to cool my heels for twenty minutes before my hosts deigned to put in an appearance. They included Jim Gracie, chairman of GEC, Mr Brazier, chairman of the Birmingham Mint, Sir Bernard Docker, of Daimler, who had a silver- or gold-studded car made for his wife, and similar celebrities used to far more prestigious mess-mates. Small fry, with nothing to recommend them but what lay between their ears, were not their flavour of the month.

I soon discovered what made industry tick because my main duty, as a member of the management board, was to sit in on industrial disputes and act as devil's advocate by posing awkward questions and arguments likely to be raised by the trades union side. When the employers in dispute had forged their case, their opponents were called into the room and the agreed case was put by the full-time official of the Employers' Federation. When impasse was reached, the two sides withdrew to have another go at cobbling up a convincing argument and the whole process was repeated till either 'agreement' or 'failure to agree' was reached and officially recorded.

The chap who often acted as devil's advocate with me was John Sully, the general manager of English Electric, and we got on fine. I gather he was a policeman's son who had made the grade to top executive, responsible for the output of 8000 employees, and he didn't mince his words or suffer fools gladly. We christened our fellows on the management board the 'Give-'em-a-whiff-of-grapeshot Gang' – and I understand we were known as the *enfants terribles*, who could be relied on for abrasive, practical advice, often very unpopular!

The conclusion I came to was that, in large firms such as Austin or Morris (it was before amalgamation into British Leyland), the union was not really interested in whether Joe Soap and his mates in the paintshop got an extra fiver a week. The object of the exercise was to get them dissatisfied enough to strike, because twenty disgruntled paint sprayers could bring a giant works to a halt, which could cause *national* political damage.

The direct labour cost of assembling a car was only a few pounds. The real cost was in millions of pounds' worth of capital equipment, so it was of no great concern to the manufacturers if the direct labour cost was doubled. It would make only a minimal addition to the selling price of a car and do less damage than a stoppage which halted income on a multi-million pound investment.

But when wages in the car industry spiral, there is a natural clamour for a similar wage in smaller firms, with a bigger proportion of direct labour cost. The inflation that results is our national curse today. The 'Give-'em-a-whiff-of-grapeshot' school too often dived for cover or shot at shadows when they should have stood their ground.

The shop-floor management at the big plants was usually impeccable and any faults generally lay with the strategy of appeasement at director level. Where small firms were concerned, Sully and I often said that, if we were there, we'd sack the gaffer and set on the shop steward, who was far more astute. As devil's advocates, however, suggesting such a course of action was not our purpose!

The jobs of spring and spring-balance making, in quantities which would have been uneconomic to mass-produce, demanded great physical skill and individual know-how. A lifetime dealing with hardened and tempered steel endowed craftsmen with experienced eyes which could predict more accurately than any impersonal computer. Salters had been founded in 1760, and some families on the shop floor could claim longer *personal* involvement with and loyalty to the company than the owners, whose control had effectively passed from godfather to unrelated godson.

When I arrived I found families whose specialist knowledge had been passed direct from father to son for almost two centuries, and I rated it a great privilege to join them, even though I was at first regarded as being 'management' – the 'wrong side of the blanket'. But the atmosphere was so like the rural hierarchy of hereditary farming communities that I really had more in common with the shop floor than the boardroom.

I regarded it as my first duty to make sure that the company made a profit, not because of any concern for share-holders but simply because I knew that any firm that doesn't run at a profit soon runs down the sough. Having made a profit, I regarded it as an equal responsibility to see that *everyone* who actively contributed to it got a fair slice of the cake.

I picked and built up the most able team I could – and delegated day-to-day decisions to them. Even if the decisions didn't come off, I always took responsibility for the failure, though I delved deep to discover why they failed and made it clear that avoidable boobs would not provide security. Decisions which I reckoned to be sensible commercial risks were always covered and initiative which succeeded was always made public so that nobody could ever say I'd scooped his credit. As a result, we really enjoyed working together, and key members of my old team still come to visit my wife and me as personal friends, although I left Salters twenty-eight years ago and they have long since retired themselves.

'The treadmill' of those years in industry was totally alien to me and I often pined for 'the simple life', but I enjoyed working at Salters all the same. I gather I was known in the works as 'a hard bugger but straight'. I could wish for no better epitaph.

FIVE

'A Bit of Clerkin''

Our top-storey flat in a Black Country high street was not the most desirable residence in which to begin married life. The weekly rent of 10 shillings (50p) was the yardstick of its value!

Having been brought up in a basically rural atmosphere, Jess naturally hated being cooped up in squalid urban surroundings, though she was far too loyal to make a thing of it. Her father was a farmer's son who had hunted, in his day, and continued shooting till well into his eighties. He was no mean exponent at the art and I once saw him, at the age of seventy-eight, bag five snipe with seven consecutive shots. I was always amazed that he welcomed me as a son-in-law when I was not a shooting man. This was not because I have anything against properly conducted country sports, but simply because I couldn't hit the proverbial bull up an entry with a gun.

I had grown up with the freedom of so many acres belonging to my Old Man's patients that I felt exactly the same as my wife about our new home. But at that time it was not done to have mortgages or buy things on the never-never. We saved up for what we wanted and did without it till there was enough in the kitty to cover the cost. Even today we never buy anything till we've saved the money to pay for it.

So our £4 a week income was pretty tight and the first job on our return from honeymoon was to sort out our expenses to see what we

could do without. I had read *The Field* every week since I had started at prep school. It brought a breath of fresh air into our urbanized surroundings – but it cost a shilling (5p) a week! We decided, reluctantly, that it would have to go. Reading the last issue very nostaligically, I came across what I regarded as a rotten article and mentioned casually that I should be glad to dump *The Field*; I could write better stuff myself. I had never written anything for publication; never even tried. So it was a silly thing to say to anyone as sharp as Jess.

'Why don't you then?' she asked. 'If you write anything decent, they'll pay you for it – and that will cover the cost of *The Field*.'

My bluff was called! It was no good back-peddling: I was stuck with it. The knife was between my ribs and she kept on prodding till, to shut her up, I wrote an article and submitted it.

The editor was then Brian Vesey-FitzGerald, a fine writer, distinguished broadcaster and a good, if contentious, naturalist. Not surprisingly, he rejected my contribution. But he did not do so with a printed rejection slip, as many of his successors would have done. He wrote a personal letter saying that it was not the material he was looking for – but he liked the style. What did I know more about than anyone else knew? Why not write about that?

I couldn't think what I knew as *much* about as anyone else, far less more. So far as I was concerned, that was the end of the matter. Not so Jess. She gave me no peace till I tried again.

The only subjects I could perhaps claim to know more about than most literate people, at least in theory, were dog-fighting and cock-fighting. I had never actually *seen* either – and never wanted to. But some of the Old Man's collier patients kept bull terriers, not for dog shows, and gamefowl, not for laying eggs.

I asked the editor if he was interested and he commissioned an article on Stafford bull terriers, for which he paid me 30 shillings (£1.50). That was enough to cover my subscription to *The Field* for the next six months. He wrote a very kind letter saying he had enjoyed the article – so now would I submit one on fighting cocks? I told him I knew much more about gamefowl than bull terriers, so would he take it in two articles? He said I'd better have a go – if only for my cheek!

That was in 1941 and I was extremely proud to write for him every few weeks for several years afterwards because *The Field*, in those days, was a highly respected and influential country journal which had immense impact on rural thinking. When Brian moved on, I wrote for every subsequent editor until 1989 when policy changed and a woman took over who seemed hell-bent on increasing circulation at any cost, even by pandering to what traditionalists regarded as 'green-welly wallies'. Along with a number of other respectable regular contributors, I declined invitations to continue writing under the new regime.

Just before Brian gave up his editorship of the magazine, he wrote to inform me he was going into book publishing. He had been commissioned to edit a series of County Books for Robert Hale and invited me to write the book on Staffordshire. He said that he knew that I had never written a book before but, before I said no, he asked me to meet him in London, and to take Jess, to discuss the proposition.

It was a red-letter day in our lives. He took us to lunch at the Authors' Club, where we saw George Bernard Shaw and other notabilities, and I returned with the promise of a contract in my pocket – and the address of his own agent to negotiate the terms. Meeting a man with no ulterior motive who was so kind and helpful was the greatest luck we had. The rest was up to us.

To my friends in the factory the idea of my writing was hilarious, because they rated nothing as work which did not make them sweat – literally. 'Messing about writing books', to their way of thinking, was just doing a bit of 'clerkin''. The next thing they expected was my turning up for work with an umbrella and *Daily Telegraph*!

That first bit of 'clerkin'' entailed settling down about nine o'clock at night and working through till one or two the next morning. I found it impossible to start as soon as I got in from work, soon after six, because I needed a meal and time to relax and unwind to rid myself of the pressures of the working day.

My book on Staffordshire was published in 1948, and Robert Hale invited me to write another of my choice in his Regional Books series, to follow it on. I chose the Black Country as my subject in this case, for I knew a great deal more about the area, where I had grown up, than I did about the county of Staffordshire as a whole; north and south Staffordshire are totally different in character. The Potteries 'belong' to Northern England and the Black Country was unique at that time, being the perfect microcosm of the dramatic changes brought about by the Industrial Revolution. The opportunity to write a book about it, to capture the personality of my region, at the moment of its disintegration, through demolition and 'redevelopment', was unique. I tried, however vainly, to stop time in its tracks to leave a thumbnail sketch. Whatever the reactions of readers to the efforts of a novice may have been, it certainly taught *me* a great deal about the changing face and character of rural England over three generations – Jess's and mine and those of our parents and grandparents, as recounted to us in childhood. St Murphy's second law, that 'All change is for the worse', was demonstrated graphically.

Brian Vesey-FitzGerald became and remained a close friend and we still keep contact with his widow. He was on the panel of speakers for Foyle's Lecture Agency – for whom I have worked for the last eighteen years – and, when he was speaking in the Midlands, he often sent us a couple of tickets, telling us to not to bother to attend the lecture, which would bore the pants off us, but to turn up at the hall and go for a drink or a meal with him afterwards. We always did go to hear him speak, because he could charm the birds off the trees.

A quarter of a century later, after watching a *Look Stranger* programme on television about my wildlife reserve, Christina Foyle paid me the compliment of inviting me to join her panel of speakers. Brian was a hard act to follow but years of experience 'on the box' had accustomed me to the frustrations of talking to disinterested microphones and deadpan cameras, which show no more reaction to eloquence than to rubbish.

So I grabbed the opportunity she offered and have now revelled in eighteen years sparking exhilarating 'feedback' which is only possible with the wide spectrum of very 'live' audiences which Miss Foyle's agency attracts.

Brian Vesey-FitzGerald had really made this possible by initiating me to the spoken word as he had to writing when he had commissioned my first contribution to *The Field*, back in 1941. 'Why don't you have a go at broadcasting?' he had asked. 'It's the hell of a good racket!' I replied that I knew nobody 'on the inside', so how did I break in?

The recipe was the same as for writing. 'If you know something the others don't,' he said, 'you're in business. It doesn't matter if it's only the articulation of a gnat's knee. You needn't even know where his ankle is. They'll give you a whirl.'

It seemed an unlikely story, but Jess kept prodding, so I wrote to BBC Midland Region saying I had heard nothing about the bull-rings and bull-stakes of the Black Country. Nor had they so, as Brian had predicted, they invited me to contribute an item of two minutes and forty-five seconds, for which they paid me two guineas (£2.10). That was in 1947 and I averaged an appearance every three weeks for the next thirteen years. I naturally concentrated on subjects which interested me, about which I had some chance of knowing at least as much as most, if not more, and I particularly enjoyed contributing items to *Countrylover*, an evocative, gentle programme presented by Freddie Grisewood, who was universally respected. I eventually inherited the programme, under the title *Countryside*, and presented it monthly. The title changed to *In the Country*, but it remained a marvellous sounding board for rural attitudes; for thirteen years it reflected both acceptable change and the areas where resistance was vital if the future was to be safeguarded.

I made friends with contemporary 'characters' who had followed the landmarks of my youth. Miss Frances Pitt, the distinguished country writer, contributed a regular weekly country column to a London paper for longer than any other journalist, from the early 1920s till within a fortnight of her death in 1961. She farmed 600 acres – in an environmentally friendly fashion – near Bridgnorth, in Shropshire, and was Master of the Wheatland Hounds. I believe she did her first and her last broadcast with me, and among our fondest memories were her famous Sunday lunches. She never sent out invitations but 'summoned' Jess and me to lunch. Refusal would have been unthinkable, because it was quite certain that fellow diners would include distinguished naturalists and writers, artists and sportsmen there was no other way of meeting.

At the other end of the social scale, I made friends with Bert Gripton, a professional earth-stopper and terrierman to a local hunt, whose job was to bolt foxes unsporting enough to go to ground when hounds got dangerously close. He was on par with Hairy Kelly, the professional ratcatcher of my youth, who was such a good naturalist I believe he really thought like this quarry, who were, therefore, that much easier to outwit. Bert was a truly formidable character and folk made an enemy of him at their peril. Rural rumour had it that members of an adjoining hunt were furious because Bert had been poaching foxes from 'their' territory, although a farmer on whose land the foxes were had given Bert permission to catch them. Complaints were passed to the hunt which employed him and, in the interests of good relations, he was sacked.

It may have been coincidence that the next eighteen days' hunting were blank, though there was a rumour that Bert had taken note of the fixture list and 'dealt with' the fox earths before hounds arrived. After he was re-employed there was no further trouble, which may also have been coincidence. Or it may not!

Another interesting character I met was Lord Rennell of Rod, the distinguished geographer, whose life's hobby had been the restoration of a medieval irrigation scheme as modern as tomorrow. There was a stream running along the lower boundary of his estate and he restored a mill leet which channelled water along a higher boundary. The stream and leet were connected by cross-dykes, controlled by sluices, so that consecutive sections of the farm could be flooded or drained at will. It made the mechanical sophistication of modern husbandry seem ridiculously complicated and wasteful.

While I was working on 'steam' radio, we did a lovely series of programmes called *Sunday Out*. They started in about 1952 and continued through the summers of '53, '54, '55 and '56. For each programme the BBC would book four contributors with differing interests into some country pub on Friday night. Bill Hartley had a car, John Moore a horse, there was often a women to give the female slant, and I was the chap who walked with his dog. Geoffrey Bright, the West Country estate agent, often 'covered' the Big House or upmarket family – and we did what we liked on Saturday and Sunday. On Sunday night the producer arrived and recorded a programme about what we had found in the area and it was transmitted the following Friday to sow seeds of inspiration for people who wished to spend a 'Sunday out' in the area.

I don't know how the customers enjoyed it, but I know I did. There is no introduction to fellow countrymen better than a good dog, so I took mine into the bar of whatever pub we were booked into on Friday night. I was soon asked by some local, who would otherwise have closed like a clam at the approach of strangers from the Beeb, and asked if Dinah my whippet-lurcher was any good. 'Can she catch one?' was usually the question. We would become instant old friends and, before closing time, I would be pointed in the direction of folk in the area it would otherwise have taken weeks to unearth. I 'found' the source of the River Welland in a rectory cellar with the help of the local milkman, who was a water-diviner in his spare time! I went 'bapping' for eels, catching them on threads of wool threaded through huge earthworms. An introduction to a fabulously rich tycoon, who 'acquired' a large estate by systematically putting his neighbours out of business by bribing their workmen to work for him, made me feel sick.

The exploitation of the countryside by shady wheeler-dealers is not a new phenomenon. The opportunities of meeting a complete cross-section of country folk, from belted earls to the chaps who poached their pheasants, were limitless. And, when it is vital to dredge up interesting and original stories within twenty-four hours of visiting an area, it certainly concentrates the mind. Broadcasters are as good – or as bad! – as their last performance, so shrinking flowers soon wilt.

I loved – and still love – working on the wireless, but I think I got the clearest insight into the basic reasons for differing types of country from another series called *A Grant of Land*. We chose a number of large estates, each of which was owned by a family with a background totally different from the others. We talked to the owners, their servants and tenants to try to deduce what effect each family had had or would have on the history of the area and its type of country in the past and in the future; whether the balance sheet was in debit or credit.

One pre-Norman family we met had done nothing spectacular and had kept up an estate of around 5000 acres for about a thousand years. It was superb, combining mixed woodland and farmland, and, although the family was not rich – except in land – they were highly territorial and guarded it against speculative developers and similar despoilers of the countryside. One might expect that landowners with such deep roots would have tenants and servants whose families had spent a similarly long time on the estate. However, we were surprised to find that this was not so, and the reason proved to be that the owners had switched from the Catholic to the Protestant faith about a century previously. At this time religion was taken so seriously that ancient families of tenants and workers had been replaced or left in protest at what they saw as disloyalty to the religion of their ancestors.

We also examined the story of a family in whose house the plan for the Battle of Edgehill was hatched, discovering that the current owner still held high political office. And, rather as the more cynical of us forecast, financial tycoons who had bought a great estate but spent the week in a city office, to make the money to run it, were a pretty unpleasant bunch. The description 'muck-and-Mercs' suited them very well.

Finally we examined what had been a large estate at the instant of its disintegration – and for personal reasons I still treasure the tape-recording of the bid on which it changed hands. This was as recently as 1963, when 1000 acres of woodland and 1000 acres of agricultural land with three cottages were knocked down for £85,000 the lot: less than a modern country 'cottage'. What is more, the purchasers paid only the deposit of £8,500 plus interest till they had broken up the estate and resold it! The reasons for my close interest were that the sale included what is now our house and wildlife reserve. I was able to buy them from the financiers, who took their cut of profit before passing it over to me.

A millionaire turkey tycoon bought the 1000-acre wood (which he could do nothing with because the Forestry Commission hold it on a

999-year lease) and about 900 acres of farmland for a reputed £60,000. Subsidies for 'improvements' went far towards grubbing out the remaining ancient oaks, draining, liming and ploughing the land and putting in a hard road for lorries to fetch the corn. He did an astute deal.

Broadcasting about such radical changes in the countryside provides unique opportunities to probe deeper into the mechanisms of change than would otherwise be possible. The area where we live, from Rugeley to Burton-upon-Trent, including most of the ancient Forest of Needwood and part of the Queen's Duchy of Lancaster estate, had, like the Dukeries of Nottingham, been safeguarded against exploitation because it comprised a number of large contiguous estates owned by hereditary landowners. They regarded it as their duty to pass on their possessions to the next generation undefiled by the 'theme parks' which are ruining the countryside in this generation.

Trendy politicians and bent bureaucrats, who obtain 'sweeteners' to grant planning permission, sneer at the old landowners for being paternalistic and obstructive to their plans – but I know which I prefer. The England of my youth was still unspoiled and beautiful. It changed with the technical advances of husbandry, which demanded bigger fields for bigger machines. But it is only in my lifetime that greed and corruption have been rotting rural guts.

I also started in television while I was at Salters, first appearing on the box in August 1952. It was long before colour and it went out live. Landing in at the deep end I had no idea of the number of rehearsals which would be needed to make sure we came out on time. I had been asked to bring my tame badger, which lived in a loosebox, came in the house when I got back from work and came for a walk with the dogs. 'Tame' is a subjective term – for badgers are anything but domesticated. Mine had arrived, as so many foundlings do, as a result of being rescued from diggers, who had killed the sow. I had bottle-reared him, so that he was fixated on me – but he didn't put up with any liberties.

After about the fourth rehearsal, he decided he'd had enough of being messed about – and he didn't like the cameramen, stage manager, sound engineers or producer. He was even getting fed up with me. So, when I bent down to pick him out of a huge packing case he had been using as a sleeping box, he rebelled – and bit me. All the camera could see was a huge expanse of Drabble posterior and all the producer could hear was language quite unfitted for broadcasting in Lord Reith's day. Luckily my badger behaved acceptably during the actual performance, so my television career did not come to a sticky end before it began.

We did quite a bit of television for children and I introduced my craftsmen friends from the Black Country who made heavy anchor chains and others who created the most beautiful, delicate table glass to delight the viewers. Something usually went wrong during these live programmes, such as when a blacksmith chopped half-way through his finger within seconds of the start and there was no certainty that the numbness would not wear off before the programme ended, leaving me to hold a conversation with a tough-looking character in a dead faint. One chap, whose Black Country dialect was so broad that it didn't matter what he said because no one could understand him, suddenly interrupted me, with great clarity, to tell me I hadn't asked him to *sing* yet! And a deer I was hand-rearing went unexpectedly berserk in front of a live audience of several hundred children. There is nothing like it to teach one not to panic but to think on one's feet!

I did quite a bit of writing during this period too. Brian Vesey-FitzGerald passed a couple more books my way, one for Penguin and one for Cassells, while I was still at Salters. Jess, who is professionally trained in domestic science – not as a secretary – laboriously typed the whole of a *Penguin Book of Pets* from my spidery handwriting.

Access to such a wide variety of countryman encouraged me to mount a series of campaigns on subjects close to my heart. I have loved badgers since reading *The Wind in the Willows* and Williamson's *Bloody Bill Brock*; and Frances Pitt had hand-reared tame badgers, otters and red squirrels, which bred freely in her attics. So when the Ministry of Agriculture, Fisheries and Food mounted a campaign to exterminate badgers in the West Country, on the spurious 'evidence' that they were the vectors spreading bovine TB among cattle, it was more than I could stand.

I discovered that most bovine TB infecting human beings in this country died out when milk began to be pasteurized and sterilized, and the 'cure' was so spectacular that many TB sanatoria were closed. It reappeared only when waves of immigrants arrived from countries where the disease is endemic, and most TB is now of a human strain, and not bovine TB at all. But bureaucrats do not advocate 'controlling' immigrants!

The disease persisted in the West Country, several times worse than elsewhere in Britain, and as ministry vets could not pinpoint the cause they continued to use badgers as the excuse. By the time the ministry campaign was eventually stopped, as a result of the Dunnet Report, I had become fairly well known at the ministry – and had learned a lot about dealing with bureaucrats.

Asking local MPs to help you with this sort of problem is often pretty useless because so many of them are so terrified of offending anyone that they play safe by running with the hare and hunting with the hounds. The thing to do is to make contact at the top, for a trait of bumbledom is to nip *any* complaint in the bud if it arises through lower ranks. But if it comes down from the top, they take it seriously. So I try to get a newspaper to accept a paid article (not a reader's letter) and I write the article as an open letter to the minister. His subordinates are then far more civil. It is also important to be totally factual, but to couch an article in such terms as to produce sharp reaction from carefully selected readers.

My experience in the poisonous peanut campaign proved the effectiveness of such tactics. I discovered that peanuts are susceptible to a particularly deadly natural mould, called aflatoxin, when they are stored in hot and humid conditions. It is so poisonous that, I gather, several Americans have died through eating peanut oil or peanut butter contaminated with it. When this was pointed out to our government, an edict was issued ordering the Ministry of Agriculture to test all peanuts imported into this country and condemn any containing a lethal dose of aflatoxin to ensure that they were not eaten by domestic stock or people. Unfortunately, no one said what was to happen to the rejects, which should obviously be destroyed. So there is nothing to stop unscrupulous dealers buying the rejects cheaply and selling them for wild bird food. It is illegal to feed a budgerigar or other cage bird on rejected peanuts, but all right to poison a robin with them!

I took this up with MAFF, who replied that they were doing their part by safeguarding the health of people and domestic stock. If I was worried about wild birds, I should contact the Ministry of the Environment. I did so, and they said that if I produced evidence that wild birds were being killed, they would look into it. But aflatoxin is a carcinogen, and the victims contracting cancer creep away to die in secret. There are not piles of feathered corpses under every bird table.

So I wrote an article for *Saga*, the old people's publication, pointing out that pensioners who spent part of their hard-won pension on peanuts for the birds might not be doing them the favour they thought they were. They might be sitting in comfort on cold winter days watching their guests poison themselves on the nuts they made sacrifices for. I assured them that my experience had been that when this kind of thing is brought to the attention of distinguished politicians, of cabinet rank, they are more likely to take it seriously than the bumblecrats they employ. So I advised writing to the Minister of Agriculture himself, marking the letter 'Personal', and also to C.J. Wildbird Foods, of Attingham, Shrewsbury, who were trying to organize concerted, responsible action by the pet-food trade.

The minister didn't tell me how many letters he received – but C.J. Wildbird Foods got no fewer than 900 from that one article in a specialist magazine. The threat of loss of votes on 'green' issues certainly produces some action!

I shall also continue to campaign vigorously against the poisons spewed upon our land in the name of 'efficient' agriculture. On one hand the politicians gripe about farmers who overproduce and make mountains of surplus corn, so they actually *pay* them to leave 'set-aside' wastes of untilled land. In the next breath the same oafs say that it is vital to produce food as efficiently and cheaply as possible, and encourage them to use the foulest pesticides, fungicides and herbicides, irrespective of the obscene side effects on wildlife and plants. This simply panders to the greed of the agrochemical industry – and perhaps lines the politicians' back pockets with sweeteners or lucrative seats on company boards. It might be far saner and more responsible to improve and increase the acreage devoted to high-quality organic farming, though it might not make so many rich men grow richer.

No government body has taken more stick from environmentalists than the Forestry Commission, which is accused of turning vast tracts of our most beautiful hill country into deserts of foreign pines, so sterile that neither animal nor plant can survive beneath the canopy of shade they cast. As I am not shy about standing up to be counted for my criticism of faceless bureaucrats, it is unsurprising that my voice has been heard crying doom upon Big Brother. But I am old enough to have lived through two world wars, the second of which I remember vividly. So I know from experience how dreadfully our native woodlands were plundered to aid the War Effort!

By the 1920s so much timber had been felled that the government saddled the Forestry Commission with the task of making good the loss. Vast acreages of softwoods were planted for two reasons. Some return on the outlay could be expected during the first thirty-five years – and slick politicians are not in favour of planting pears (or other slow-growing hardwoods) for their heirs. They may be out of office by the time the crop matures. They prefer a crop which has a fair chance of ripening before they are cast into the political wilderness. An even more practical reason for planting softwoods is that they act as a nurse-crop for interplanted or self-regenerated native trees, which are 'drawn up' by the adjacent shady pines like daffodils in a dark cupboard. When the nurse-crop is thinned and later felled, the hardwoods among them branch out and grow strong. So the initial mass-planting of pinewoods was highly practical, however badly it nettled the purists who are deluded that the environment can survive without change. Timber is as much a crop as corn, to be sown and harvested in an ultra-slow rotation as it matures and ripens.

Far more scandalous, to my eyes as a dedicated naturalist, was the Forestry Commission's treatment of wildlife. The hidebound traditionalists among them had no greys. Everything was clear-cut black and white; a friend or foe of trees. Foes, whatever they were, whether deer or rabbits, hares or squirrels, damaged trees at some stage and should, therefore, be exterminated as gamekeepers killed hawks and owls. Even badgers were for the chop, not because they caused direct damage but because they rooted up the wire-netting surrounding crops of young trees – and let the rabbits creep in where they had made a gap.

Country lovers were so much up in arms that, in sheer self-defence, the commission decided to clean up its image. Such public relations exercises were not common just after the last war, but Herbert Fooks was hired to spearhead one. He did not find it easy, because foresters of the old school regarded growing trees as their job in life. Anything that interfered with that was not to be tolerated.

One man saw sense in what Fooks had been set to do and he offered to help. He was Jack Chard, conservator at Chester and responsible for forests in almost a fifth of England, an area stretching southwards from the Lake District, along the Welsh border to the West Country, with Cannock Chase and woodlands in North Staffordshire, Worcestershire and Shakespeare's Forest of Arden thrown in for good measure. I had known Jack for years as we were founder members of the Mammal and Deer Societies, and, knowing what a keen naturalist he was, I was not surprised by his co-operation.

The treatment of deer in Forestry Commission territory had caused particularly deep resentment among the public: driving deer to waiting shotguns, shooting at them indiscriminately, collecting the fallen and leaving cripples to creep away to die in agony. Fooks decreed that it must stop forthwith. He had been in charge of a wildlife reserve in Africa and was currently employed to manage game and wildlife on royal estates, so he knew the nuts and bolts of the job. He decided to cause a census to be taken of the wild deer in each forest, together with a survey of the available keep, to assess the head of deer that could be carried without unacceptable damage. High seats, or observation platforms on stilts, were erected so that surplus deer could be selectively shot, the worst specimens being chosen for culling. The survivors would then be the fittest, to improve the quality of the herd, instead of the best being taken as 'trophies', leaving rubbish to breed the following year.

Fooks asked Jack Chard to send a trainee to improve the quality and the lot of the deer, and he chose Gerald Springthorpe, the warrener at Cannock Chase and an old personal friend of mine, because he was such a good naturalist. He proved to be a natural for the job and was stationed at Cannock where he trained the game wardens of other forests.

Jack Chard was naturally delighted with his protégé and gave him an unconventionally free hand. He also trained Bill Grant, chief forester of Grisedale, who subsequently made Grisedale a showpiece of progressive conservation, even establishing a 'Theatre in the Forest' which draws artists from all over the world and theatregoers who are willing to time holidays to dovetail with the particular show they wish to see. Exhibitions of rural crafts and works of art are also held there.

Meanwhile Gerald Springthorpe not only improved the deer herd at Cannock, but also co-operated with bird watchers and made areas for butterflies, native orchids and other plants. He created areas for lizards and snakes, because although urban visitors may be less attracted by them, they are native species and notices asking the public not to disturb them do much to reduce human pressure on other species. They encourage people to go elsewhere, so removing pressure on sensitive areas, and reducing damage. Gerald started as a tractor driver at Cannock and climbed the ladder of promotion until he became an acknowledged expert whose advice is sought by great landowners in this country, Ireland and in Germany; I know of nobody who has dedicated his life more to conservation nor done more for the public relations of the Forestry Commission.

When Dilys Breese made a feature television programme about his work at Cannock, his management of shy species was so efficient that we were able to capture on film a wide selection, from adders to foxes and deer, showing pools, 'deer lawns' and wide rides. These serve the dual purpose of encouraging deer to feed towards the centre of the forest, far from farm crops they might damage, and providing, at the same time, a chance for members of the public to derive quiet enjoyment in watching them.

'Managing' wildlife was not Gerald's only problem. Shy species thrive on a sense of security, just as we do, and large, rumbustious parties scare off everything within earshot. So he 'managed' visitors by creating suitable habitat for adders in areas where minimum disturbance was vital. A few notices saying 'Please do not step on the adders' caused no offence but restricted visitors to the knowledgeable enthusiasts – who would cause no disturbance anyway!

So by no means all my conservation articles were critical because I feel it equally important to give credit where it is due by alerting readers, viewers and listeners to the fact that there may be more people than they suppose who also care about the countryside we leave for future generations. Nothing demonstrates this better than the fact that, although he no longer works for the Forestry Commission, to whom he gave the best part of his life, Gerald is still producing astonishingly spectacular rabbits out of his wildlife-management hat.

Sadly, he had to take early retirement because he contracted tinnitus, probably as a result of an industrial accident at work, and could no longer disentangle several voices in unison at meetings and conferences. It happened like this. The commission allows 'licensed shooters' (one can scarcely call them 'sportsmen') to shoot selected deer for a fee. They have to be accompanied by a warden, who selects which deer they shoot to ensure the commission policy of improving the herd by leaving the best bucks to breed and culling the worst. Gerald's client was a Hun who saw a buck he wanted and did not wait for permission but raised his rifle and shot it. The explosion was near Gerald's ear and his hearing has never been right since. He reported the accident but the report was burned in a fire which wrecked the forest office, so that there is no hard evidence that he reported it. Once such sordid incidents get into the hands of lawyers, leeches are outleeched, for the longer a case lasts, the higher the legal costs and fees. In our enterprise society, ethics stand little chance against greed, whoever is at the thick end of the stick.

Gerald's latest triumph is with kingfishers which haunt the stream running beside his retirement cottage. He cut vertical faces to the banks, creating artificial 'cliffs' which he bored with horizontal tunnels at carefully selected sites. For the last two years kingfishers have taken to the tunnels as readily as tits to a nestbox, and reared their annual brood successfully. The icing on the cake is that he has sited the artificial nest sites strategically so that they are perfect background for photography from a permanent 'hide' quite close to the house.

The purpose of the artificial 'cliffs' is to deter marauding mink, stupidly 'liberated' a few years ago from a local mink ranch by trendy activists. The escapees that have survived have colonized the area and are wreaking havoc among waterfowl and small birds, including kingfishers, whose nests they rob whenever possible. Gerald keeps tunnel traps set on regular tracks to catch invading mink as keepers catch stoats and weasels. They would have had a more comfortable death if the do-gooders had left them in the mink ranch. But usually the mink cannot climb vertical banks to reach the nest holes bored into them.

A wide range of radio and television programmes, twenty-odd books and general journalism have enabled me to make a magnum of friends of like mind who have greatly enriched our lives. I love playing with words – and am not averse to controversy – and have deliberately tested the water to discover which country pleasures and threats to rural life motivate people most; because, to have a real chance of protecting the countryside effectively in the future, it is absolutely vital to know the most sensitive areas to prod. But it often happens that readers and editors and I all laugh or cry at totally different things.

Regular columns in papers can have considerable influence on what readers will lobby MPs about, so it is essential to understand the tastes of the readers. When I started a regular weekly column in the *Birmingham Evening Mail* in 1964, it was a deeply respected newspaper which wielded significant political clout. It eventually fell into the hands of foreign owners and I received a letter from the editor terminating my column – after twenty-six years – because his *'research had shown that the countryside holds little interest'* (my italics). He went on to say, 'I doubt if many of my readers would recognize a wren and their idea of a dawn chorus is the milkman whistling on his rounds.'

If he is right, it is a pretty depressing prospect for the future of the countryside and, if he really has to grovel to 'win back readers in our heartland: Birmingham city itself', the influence of previously respected newspapers hardly encourages optimism. Fortunately, I think he under-rates his readers, for my experience in other fields suggests that more and more people are getting fed-up with the heartlands of big cities and yearn for the deeper values of the countryside instead.

In 1975 I was invited by a distinguished London BBC television producer to present a series of programmes about sheep-dog trials under the title of *One Man and his Dog*. I declined at first because I thought that sheep-dog trials were too repetitive and specialist to attract casual viewers. I thought they might enjoy *one* programme, showing what it was all about, but after that I expected them to drop off their perch with boredom.

The producer differed in his opinion. He had already found Eric Halsall to do the commentaries and Eric ate, drank, slept and waked sheep dogs and sheep-dog trials. He had forgotten more about them than most of us will ever know. His enthusiasm bubbled from every pore and it was impossible not to be infected by his commentary. We hit it off the first time we met and we got on even better at every subsequent encounter.

The producer took on board my doubts but countered them by saying that each programme would have as background superb views of stunning scenery. The result has been that casual viewers, switching on or letting the set run on after the previous programme, are riveted to their seats by the sight of dramatic views of Lakeland or the peace and seclusion of the best 'man-made' country in the world in such estates as Chatsworth, the home of the Duke and Duchess of Devonshire.

The shepherds themselves, spending solitary lives with their dogs and flocks in lonely, wild hill country, come across as the real men they are: dignified, capable craftsmen in the ancient arts of stockmanship whom viewers feel it a real privilege to meet. And they really *do* meet them, because we make a short film of each competitor at home, so that viewers feel they know the family where Mum makes cakes for the WI or the kids rear cade lambs on the bottle or play with delightful sheep-dog pups 'destined', Eric says, 'to grow into the wisest dogs on earth'. The result is that when the man we filmed at home comes on to the trials field with his dog, viewers feel he is an old and valued friend, not some impersonal competitor. They root for him in his trial, sharing his successes and mourning bad luck, when it strikes, for the trials contain both luck and judgement.

All nice people like nice dogs, especially clever ones which will do what their dog won't, and when performance is tinged with competition, it puts the icing on the cake. Proof of this theory lies in the fact that the programme is still running after fifteen consecutive years. It is seen in Ireland, America, Japan and on the continent, though some of the more trendy BBC top brass have tried to kill it. When it was last threatened because it was considered old hat, viewer reaction was violent. *One Man and his Dog* is a refreshing change from the incessant sex, violence and politics spewed over our television screens. Nice people obviously enjoy it because it is wholesome and feeds their nostalgia for the deep values of true country folk, for a life in which craftsmanship has not yet been obliterated by the wonders of our technological revolution. The simple values and security of real country are not the shifty fantasies trendy-Wendies pretend.

Working for the programme is equally attractive. Ian Smith, the producer, is the sort of leader who naturally inspires loyalty. He manipulates a seven-camera crew of more than forty with no back-biting or needling. We do eight programmes in five and a half days, which is the hardest work I've ever done, as I am not geared to concentrating so hard for so long. Yet, each September for fifteen years, I have met competitors and crew who all *want* to be there, come rain or shine (and it can rain in those hills!), and when we go home at the end of the week we are all infinitely richer, not financially but for the experience we have gained.

When I get depressed by 'knocking' journalism and squalid, immoral boffins and politicians, who are anxious to prostitute the countryside for greed, I can regain my sanity, not by counting sheep going into the fold, but by totting up the number of truly delightful people I have met while working on that programme. There are even more of them than sheep!

SIX

ESCAPE

Although my friends in the works still regarded my writing and broadcasting as an eccentric bit of 'clerkin'', the fact was that the tail which had been my escapist hobby gradually began to wag the dog. 'Work' had not yet become a dirty word, but by 1960 I was taking so many odd days off to go broadcasting, do research or interviews or meet publishers and producers that I forfeited the whole of my 'official' fortnight's holiday, which was all even directors took in those days.

I had already taken the first steps towards 'getting away from it all' by buying a cottage in the country and commuting 20 miles to work. It had nothing to do with the conventional status symbols of success but was triggered by my instinctive nostalgia for the seclusion and rural values of my fathers. Directors of large companies are, in my view, paid far more than they are worth, so that the 'cottage' we were able to afford was a pleasant half-timbered house with a pool and mill stream, flanking 10 acres of paddock on the fringe of a village.

But the higher you climb, the further there is to fall, and the internal politics, potential take-overs and redundancies of this enterprise society have made security and probity as superfluous as other civilized values. The illusion of fellow commuters that, when we reached the shelter of our village home at night, we were as inviolate as ancient fugitives seeking sanctuary in holy places was comforting, if illusory.

I had one major advantage. My mushrooming hobby might offer a

better hole to go to than more conventional alternative employment. I had made enough pals on the Old Boy Network to enable me to leave industry to become my own master and earn my living with my pen – in theory. The decision to do so was the most momentous of our lives and Jess and I mulled it over endlessly. We had always lived within our means, having no debts or mortgage so that we need not live *quite* hand to mouth. It would not be death and disaster if I went a few weeks without a commission. But once writers and broadcasters are forced to go cap-in-hand for work, the inference is that they have got the skids under them and they are no longer assets but liabilities. We were not worried about that – at least for a while – and folk I had worked for as a hobby seemed happy to use my services professionally.

So in 1961, at the age of forty-seven, I burned my boats and left Salters, knowing only too well that, if my ink ran dry, my chances of retrieving a similar status in industry were pretty slim. It was a gut-churning time, and Jess and I experienced at first hand the sense of insecurity which drives so many urban workers back to seek peace in the countryside their ancestors left in the Industrial Revolution.

It was no coincidence that I started off with an unusual combination of knowledge. The Old Man had wanted me to join the medico-legal profession because of its scarcity value. Brian Vesey-FitzGerald had advised writing about anything I knew more about than my competitors; I have always been open to good advice, so I delved in my mind for a nugget of wisdom. I didn't strike gold – but it did occur to me that not too many naturalists had nitty-gritty pragmatic minds, developed by competitive, commercial in-fighting. And not too many industrialists knew a bull from a bulrush. Perhaps I could cash in on that?

Now that it was no longer vital to commute to the big city every day, in all weathers, we could move further out, to *real* country, as opposed to the commuter belt. We could trade in the 'desirable' cottage, on the edge of an accessible village, for an isolated place where demand would be less because the type of executive who might otherwise have liked it could not afford to be marooned by fog or snow in winter. There might be someone else at his desk when he got back to the office!

The sort of place we really wanted would be in the centre of a large estate where landowners had protected their land from the developers for generations. Sadly, the only opportunity to acquire such property is when an estate is broken up by death duties or other calamity. My work in rural journalism, over the years, had enabled me to get around the Midland countryside to places where the public does not normally penetrate so that, when I heard that the Bagot estate, near Abbots Bromley, would shortly fall under the hammer, I was more than interested.

The sale was in the village pub in September of 1962. I covered it for BBC News, making a tape-recording of the bid which knocked it down, and eventually managed to buy our cottage and 90 acres of woodland a mile outside the village. The house is a folly, built by the landowner 150 years ago to enhance the entrance to his park and to house the goatherd who tended the family's historic herd of goats. These were said to have originated as milk and meat on the hoof during the time of the Crusades. The cottage was called Goat Lodge.

It was pretty rough, to put it mildly, when we bought it – we could not have afforded it otherwise. One stark cold-water tap delivered piped water to the scullery sink. That was the only mod. con. There wasn't even a drain to take the water away; just a pipe from the sink, jutting out over the garden. The nearest electricity was at the farm a quarter of a mile away; there was no bathroom and the earth closet, a friendly two-seater, was across the yard on the far side of a huge bed of stinging nettles. Being taken short in the dark must have been a hazardous experience. What had once been a small garden was now a dense jungle of hawthorn scrub, and the front door opened into the parlour, which was next to the kitchen. Not surprisingly, there was little competition for the place and, after endless legal wrangles, we bought it very cheaply.

The 90 acres of woodland that we acquired simultaneously comprised a 30-acre oak wood, with a heronry of eighteen nests – and a felling licence to sell the timber of the trees which housed the nests! About 40 acres of other standing timber had just been felled – and the land it had stood on was let to the Forestry Commission for 999 years at half a crown ($12\frac{1}{2}$p) an acre! The rest comprised three pools and odd paddocks and patches of pasture.

Before clinching the deal it was necessary to know if we could get planning consent to enlarge the cottage which looked fine from outside but would have been quite impossible to modernize properly without major alterations – and it was a listed building. I went to see the county planning officer, who seemed less concerned about what I wanted to do with the house than by whether I intended to use the licence to fell the trees containing the heronry. Local ornithologists, including the son-in-law of the director of the Nature Conservancy, were pressing for a Tree Preservation Order to preserve the trees containing the nests. Local planners had no power to oblige because the wood was controlled by the Forestry Commission, who had issued the licence to fell.

I said that *I* should not use a licence to fell the trees because I was more interested in the heronry. Thereafter the planners were most helpful because planners, in those golden days, were more interested in protecting the countryside against incompatible development than in planning gain, which is some financial advantage wrung from the developer as the price of consent to develop. All too often, I suspect, planning gain is really planners' gain in the shape of untraceable sweeteners to grease the back pockets of potentially 'bendable' boffins and bureaucrats.

I shall never forget the excitement when it was eventually confirmed that Jess and I really owned the sort of place we would have given our eye teeth to visit on holiday for almost a quarter of a century in the industrial rat race. We wandered round it together, at dusk and dawn, taking a census of our fellow residents. There were fallow deer, terrified by our approach because they had never before met people who did not let off a charge of shot at any deer foolish enough to hang around within range of a shotgun. There were hawks and owls, redstarts and grasshopper warblers, badgers and herons, woodpeckers and woodcock, nightjars and wrens and tits and finches. They would have worn out the black lead in any twitcher's pencil.

For a while our pleasure was just escapism, but I am too much of a realist to day-dream for long. It dawned on Jess and me that we really owned a bit of England – and it was, therefore, our bounden duty to leave it better than we found it. But how?

The privilege of owning irreplaceable, shrinking habitat should never be divorced from the solemn responsibility of good stewardship. We shouldn't be here if it had not been for the herons, because it was their need for protection which encouraged the county planning officer to be so helpful. What they needed most was to feel secure; for when we went into the wood, we found young yobbos heaving stones up to the nests or climbing the trees to steal the eggs. Even innocent visitors enjoying the wild flowers and peaceful atmosphere were treated as potential enemies by the old herons, who were unable to distinguish between armed foes and inquisitive friends. So they circled aloft out of gunshot range. Before they summoned courage to return, the carrion crows, which are instinctive opportunists, nipped in and stole their eggs or savaged their young chicks.

The answer seemed to be to prevent disturbance, by either friend or foe, so that Nature could take her course and allow the birds to gain the confidence to defend their own eggs and young. At the time we had an Alsatian named Tough, which I had bought as a pup from the police after a television programme on police dogs. She was delighted to enter into the spirit of the game. I knew when there were strangers about because herons circled high overhead with loud honks of protest. I then sent Tough into the wood, where she hunted out intruders and bayed menacingly round them, preventing escape, till I went up to 'liberate' them. I enquired where they got in and where they were going before ejecting them on the further side of the wood, as far as possible from their destination, so that they had to make several miles' detour to get back. Few returned for an encore.

We were, of course, perfectly happy to take our own medicine and, even now, we do not enter Holly Covert, where the heronry is situated, between March, when the birds assemble, and May, when the chicks are too large for predation by crows.

This simple wildlife management is really no more than providing a sense of security, because neither man nor beast can thrive without it. As a direct result of thus creating a sanctuary for birds, as opposed to birdwatchers, 'our' heronry has increased, under our stewardship, from eighteen nests to 106, which represents about 2 per cent of the national heron population.

It has also been necessary to be pretty hard-faced with more conventional human predators. Soon after we came, a conversation in the local pub, apparently staged for my benefit, disclosed that the bailiff on the local reservoir had shot nineteen herons for raiding his trout. He boasted about it loudly to his friends, so that I could not help overhearing. Although herons were not, at the time, legally protected, public opinion was pressing for action on what was increasingly rated as anti-social behaviour. So I wrote an article about the bailiff's feat and covered it on BBC News. Water authorities are hyper-sensitive to such public odium and the effect was dramatic. The bailiff shot no more (at least publicly) and they sent me 1000 spawning perch, which are predators of trout, 'to keep my hungry brutes at home'.

The fact is that, if unnatural concentrations of semi-tame trout are reared for fishermen not skilled enough to catch wild fish, it is not surprising if their natural predators (such as herons) regard such heavily stocked water as tomtits regard the nuts upon a bird table. In fact subsequent analysis of the undigested food pellets below the herons' nests revealed that an astonishingly high proportion of their diet contained hair not scales. They catch moles at dusk and dawn, when they come on the surface 'worming', and there are also remains of rats, water rats and voles among their pellets. So far as the fishy portion of their diet goes, a great deal is made up of perch and eels, both of which are predatory on trout.

The bailiff and I now have an excellent relationship, but I find the attitude of commercially orientated outsiders far more sinister. When it was announced that 'my' herons nests had increased recently, I received a letter from a man who wrote: 'I am also keen on conservation, *to a limit* [my italics]. I can never understand why you think it is all right for your herons to ravish the fish stock in a reservoir and prevent your neighbours stocking their pools with fish, as I would like to do, but, if anyone as much as farts within 100 yards of their nests, you get terribly incensed.'

I took the trouble to investigate my correspondent's background and to discover how keen on fishing he was. He turned out to be yet another very rich man, living 50 miles from the pools he wishes to stock – and he is not even a fisherman himself! It is the old story of much wanting more. The reason it has proved necessary to give herons legal protection is to safeguard their future from greedy enterpreneurs who are prepared to vandalize precious countryside not for their own sport but for short-term gain at whatever long-term cost.

On a far pleasanter note, we also had a few problems with the local hunt soon after we came. Hearing a row in the wood, I went out to investigate and found hounds scattering the deer in all directions, so I told the huntsman to get them out – fast! He declined, saying they had followed their hunted fox into the wood and were legally entitled to pursue it, which I knew to be perfectly true. (They would *not* be entitled to enter the wood to find and hunt a *fresh* fox there without the owner's consent.) Farmer neighbours do not like deer in their crops and I do my best to see that mine do not offend, so I repeated my request to the huntsman, who still defied me. He was within his legal rights.

I returned to the house, collected my rifle and put a bullet in the breech in full view of my uninvited guest. 'Now are you going to take them out?' I asked. He promptly obliged.

A few days later an upmarket gent arrived and introduced himself as the master of hounds, asking what my attitude to fox-hunting was.

'I think it a splendid sport,' I said. 'Why?'

'Because I am told you got out a rifle to my hounds on Saturday,' he said, 'and ordered them off your property.'

'Quite true,' I answered. 'But they were hunting deer, not foxes.'

Pained by what he mistook for my urban ignorance, he explained, in basic language, that if hunting hounds run among deer, some may riot and chase the deer instead. It is their nature.

I said that *my* hobby had been ratting, and if a farmer had invited me for a day's ratting but my terrier had killed the house cat, I should not be asked again. For my part, I would always find him a fox if his hounds were steady to deer and did not disturb them. If he couldn't control them, please would he keep them out of my wood. He accepted my reply as reasonable and kept them out for the rest of the season.

The following September I looked out of my window and saw a couple and a half of hounds hunting across an open ride. The meet was about 3 miles away, so I jumped in the car, found the master and told him hounds were rioting in my wood again. He promised to send the whip for them right away.

Nothing had happened three hours later except that my short fuse had blown. So I caught the hounds, put them in a dog pen and awaited developments. The master eventually turned up and asked where hounds were when I saw them.

'Up that ride,' I replied.

'Where did they go then?'

'They came down this way,' I said.

'And then where did they go?'

'Into that dog pen.'

It was his turn to blow a gasket then, and he said it was the first time in his life his hounds had been impounded while they were hunting. How did I catch them?

I told him, 'They chased the deer round a couple of times and then fell down exhausted. So I picked them up to give them a rest!'

We parted with mutual respect; he asked me to his hunt supporters' dinner and introduced me as the only man who ever impounded his hounds. I said I could catch them only becuse they were so unfit! It demonstrated that there is room in the countryside for the widest range of interest – if there is sensible give and take. We subsequently got on fine.

The novelty of escaping from the urban rat race to 'get away from it all to a place in the country' eventually wore off for me. I felt the need to make a more positive contribution as the naturalist I am at heart. My mind harked back to Mr Hannam, the Old Squire's head keeper, who had used his skills to produce an artificially high density of pheasants and other game for his master and his guests to shoot. His game-keeping techniques were perfectly simple. Priority number one was to avoid disturbance and to provide seclusion, to give the creatures the sense of security they needed in order to thrive. He then 'managed' the habitat so as to produce attractive food plants and safe breeding cover, and he 'controlled' the predators as necessary – far more harshly than was necessary, in my view.

It occurred to Jess and me that it might be equally possible to increase the density of any targeted species of wildlife by the same means. The surplus would then spill over into the surrounding countryside where people could enjoy it without imposing too much stress and pressure by the sheer volume of human intrusion.

Jess and I mulled it over and decided that, if we could succeed in 'managing' the wildlife in our wood, as keepers manage pheasants on a shoot, the surplus could populate the area around. It would be a satisfying way of putting something back into life, which had been very good to us, and we spent the next seven years doing experiments and investigations to improve the lot of a whole spectrum of wildlife species which shared the wood.

The year 1970 was declared to be European Conservation Year, and the Countryside Commission announced that they would give 100 Countryside Awards for projects which had 'produced some physical improvement to the countryside of England or increased the awareness and understanding of the Countryside'. This included setting up nature reserves, nature trails, country parks, field study centres, tree planting, and restoration. There were 472 submissions and all but three of the 100 awards went to corporate bodies, like the Coal Board for landscaping old pits, the CEGB for educational nature reserves, or to conservation trusts. Our wildlife reserve at Goat Lodge was one of the three 'private' winners. To enter for the award I was required to submit a paper to describe my work and part of the introduction stated:

The concept of a practical plan which would allow threatened species to breed in peace so successfully that the surplus would overspill so that the public could enjoy them without threatening them, had been practised in my reserve for six years *before* European Conservation Year, in 1970.

Re-reading my paper, I derive great comfort from the fact that the same sentiments, expressed today, would be abreast of modern theories of creative conservation, although I wrote it twenty years ago.

That Countryside Award was the milestone which marked the boundary between the urban rat race, from which we had escaped seven years before, and an exciting and a more positive contribution to the countryside we love.

All we had really done in our wildlife reserve was to confirm the fact that management and manipulation of habitat could produce an artificially high density of species, as Mr Hannam and his predecessors had done for generations. Our interests lay not in specializing on only one species, however – for pheasants came towards the bottom of our list of feathered favourites. Our ambition was to encourage as wide a variety of animals and birds, flowers and insects as could be persuaded to settle in our wood. If they were shy and persecuted, as herons and badgers are, so much the better.

To attract a variety of wildlife to the wood it would be necessary to produce as wide a variety of habitat as possible, because different species have different needs. The first thing we did was to engage contractors to cut three open woodland rides, radiating from my study window and each cleaving a swath about half a mile long through the wood to the north east, due east, and south of east. It is well known that a high proportion of woodland wildlife perfers to remain within 200 yards of the woodland edge, where there is the best light, air and space, leaving denser thickets for cover. So, by cutting these three rides, each having *two* sides abutting the trees, we were effectively creating 3 extra linear miles of productive woodland edge, which, with luck and seclusion, should attract creatures which had found no previous attractions.

The cream on the cake was that, since each ride was 'pointing' at the study and sitting-room windows, we could look deep into three sectors of the wood. Spending a great many hours at my desk, I write for about five minutes in the hour and think what I'm going to say for fifty-five – or so it seems! So any movement across a ride catches my eye (while I'm thinking) and I know where to go if I wish to get a closer look or where to avoid if it is vital not to cause disturbance. Apart from their attraction to a wide spectrum of species, those rides are literally worth hundreds of hours' fieldwork to me every year. They have repaid the cost of cutting them many times over, because they provide personal, anecdotal material about which to write and broadcast that gives me an edge over folk who are more specialized in smaller fields or recount the work of others. They help me follow Brian Vesey-FitzGerald's dictum that it is sensible to know more about something than your competitors know. Even more important, the guests which share the wood give us endless pleasure.

Twenty-odd years in the engineering industry taught me the virtues of having the proper tools for the job. Capital equipment, once acquired, can soon offset continual intensive labour costs. But, being a frugal chap, I did not lash out wildly! I bought a 1957 Ferguson 35 tractor, which was then only seven years old, for £100. These old 'Grey Fergie' diesels are almost indestructible, so that now, after a quarter of a century and one overhaul, it is as good as when I bought it – and would fetch many times what I gave for it. Agriculture has become so much more mechanized that all my farming friends have bought juggernaut machines, capable of cavorting around on the 100-acre featureless prairies which are modern fields.

The trend towards ever-larger machinery has meant that a number of other small-scale pieces of equipment have easily come my way. An ancient old single-furrow plough buries the foot of wire-netting fences, to prevent stray dogs nosing their way underneath. An old 'scuffle' breaks up rough ground, while disc and chain harrows cultivate rides to leave sweet grazing for the deer. This seduces them away from more vulnerable young trees, trying to regenerate in the wood. An old grass-topper removes coarse growth in rides and clearings and a heavy chain-swipe bashes and batters unwanted bracken to extinction. All were passed on by my farmer friends or bought very cheaply from scrappies or government surplus sales.

Our local blacksmith, a craftsman to his fingertips, made me a roller, which can be filled with water or run empty to vary the weight from about 5 cwt to more than a ton. When the worst bracken has been tamed by a thrashing from the chain-swipe, tender growth, trying to replace it, can be squashed into oblivion with the roller.

The habitat of nature reserves is commonly 'managed', more or less, by squads of volunteers from the local wildlife trust spending long weekends and sweaty summer evenings with scythes and bill hooks. I can do the same job – and more – myself, perched in comfort on my faithful old Grey Fergie. I often wonder why conservation societies don't use the cash they raise by coffee mornings, raffles and sponsored walks to kit themselves out with old but serviceable tools to mechanize the job of managing reserves they acquire. I have spent the ensuing twenty years filling my life with pleasure doing just that, though by no means all the purists approve, among them those who favour the establishment of Sites of Special Scientific Interest. The concept of these sites, which receive the blessing and (some) protection from the Nature Conservancy Council, is that they are not considered 'interesting' to scientists until some plant or species is discovered there which is either rare or of specific interest to some introspective specialist.

One woman who came to our reserve had a list of qualifications like a parish register – but all she seemed to care about was an insect about as big as a cat flea called *Cid bilamminatum*, I think it was. Ancestors of this creature, which was Specially, Scientifically Uninteresting to my eyes, had come into the country at the turn of the century with plant specimens imported to Kew Gardens. The tiny beetle thrived only in the bracket fungus on birch trees, and, since birch trees are considered a forest weed, nobody bothered to 'control' a fungus which killed them. The beetle had therefore survived and spread. The scientist who honoured us with her presence had been awarded a doctorate of philosophy for mapping its spread from Kew; it was a copybook example of how introduced species colonize the country if nobody controls them.

I myself, however, am far more interested in trying to perpetuate creatures which we take for granted because they are common today, but which may disappear in a few generations if nobody makes an effort to conserve them. And, as I would like to do this on as wide a scale as possible, I try to manage our reserve so as to get the widest possible spectrum of habitat there.

Some purists argue that this is wrong because they believe ancient habitat should remain unchanged. They refuse to recognize that, do what they will, the countryside *is* changing; it always has been in a state of change and nothing we can do will prevent it changing in the future. Time never has stood still and it never will.

It is sometimes impossible to prevent a motorway or new town or other 'essential' development destroying a colony of orchids or a badger sett, because every alternative would wreak even worse havoc. It then seems reasonable to remove the colony of orchids or persuade the colony of badgers to move themselves before the development takes place. I have a lovely colony of water soldiers in one of the pools in our wood. They were given to me, before they were legally protected, by a listener to one of my radio programmes – and I believe the first prosecution under the Wildlife and Countryside Act was for moving water soldiers without the blessing of bureaucracy. I would suffer no sleepless nights about such a 'crime', provided I did not denude the site they came from, because it seems more sensible to me to transfer threatened wildlife to areas where it will be safe than to leave it on some tiny island site where it will live in constant peril.

I was sorry to see hedgerows grubbed out to make large enough fields for modern agricultural machinery to be viable – but it was an inevitable consequence of our technological age. Responsible farmers have replanted odd corners and patches which were difficult to cultivate profitably – and I don't imagine wildlife worries whether nesting and feeding habitat is in straight lines or clumps! The farmer who bought the deerpark next to our wood grubbed out the ancient trees and spinneys to make a profitable prairie of plough, so it gave us great pleasure to plant a hedge of hawthorn and blackthorn along the woodland edge of the heronry. The oak canopy and browsing by deer from a neighbour's wood made life for the hedge pretty difficult, so that it has taken years to show signs of thriving. But the effort gave us pleasure, and gradual thickening, especially among the blackthorn, which has suckered well, raises our hopes of seeing the first nesting bird bring off a brood of young successfully!

Variety has been the keynote of our efforts. I knew that if ideal habitat for almost *any* species were provided, there was a chance that occupants would arrive as surely as tomtits to a nest box. So I started to zone the wood, providing open spaces and dense cover, food plants and thickets. It was like playing draughts, with each move years ahead, like those of old-time architects of the countryside, on a grander scale, when they 'planted pears for their heirs'.

There was a famine of dense bottom cover throughout the whole wood because the historic herd of Bagot goats had roamed the estate for centuries, creating desert conditions wherever they tarried. I often wished them in perdition. The only thing they wouldn't eat was wiry feg grass, and seeds or acorns falling on it sprouted roots in the first wet weather – but withered and died in the next dry spell so that young trees or shrubs – even bramble – were conspicuous by their absence.

It occurred to me one day that a great deal of native, mixed English woodland must owe much of its character to pigs. Commoners in the New Forest still have the Right of Pannage and can turn pigs loose there to mop up the surplus acorns. This custom was not established for any charitable reason but because horses and cattle suffer from acorn poisoning if they eat too many, while pigs thrive on them.

Too great a density of pigs will root up the ground and leave it as desolate as a ploughed field. But odd pigs, wandering haphazardly might do no damage. So each May I put three young pigs in the 30 acres of Holly Covert, where the herons are, and take them out about November, when they have cleared the surplus of the acorn fall. They turn over small, random patches, a yard or so across, and wander on till their superbly sensitive noses lead them to another likely spot.

Where they have been, the feg is uprooted and the soil beneath is left as the perfect tilth for any seeds to germinate. Patches of wood sage and bramble, bilberry and nettle appear where nothing but feg had been before. Young oak trees sprout from acorns, nut bushes from hazels and, for the first time for more than a century, there are hopes that the name Holly Covert will truly reflect its vegetation.

Purists objected to my pig scheme because, they said, it is wrong to interfere with the woodland floor, which is 'semi-natural' ancient forest – whatever that may be. Mixed woodland, with pigs as a management tool, has been subject to a variety of techniques since Man first made clearings for settlements in the woodland which once covered most of the land.

The basic love of stockmanship of native Black Countrymen has encouraged us to be as self-supporting as we can. During more than fifty years of marriage, we have never bought an egg because we have always kept free-range hens, and we buy twenty-five day-old cock chicks every year to rear as free-range birds for our table and as Christmas presents for a few personal friends. There is as much difference between the quality and flavour of these birds and intensively reared supermarket mush as between free-range and battery-produced eggs.

We get what pheasants we want out of the wood and I steal the eggs of a Canada goose, which nests on the island, and replace them with a clutch laid by a domestic goose. So our Christmas goose has been reared free for many years, since domestic geese are too heavy to accompany the wild Canadas when they fly off to flock in autumn. In just one exceptional year, 'our' geese were so aerobatic that they sailed off like helicopters with their foster parents in autumn – and the joke was unquestionably on us!

By the early 1980s I had proved my theories that, if suitable habitat is provided, it is likely to attract species that would not otherwise be there, and that skilled habitat management really can provide such an artificially high density of targeted species that there will be a surplus to overspill into the surrounding countryside. Although I could demonstrate that my techniques worked, nobody was very interested, because it was said that I was so engrossed with conservation that I worked hard all the hours God sent, took no holidays and used what profit I made from my pen to pay for the upkeep of the reserve.

The criticism had more than a grain of truth, which I accepted, so I determined to make the reserve self-financing. I called in contractors to fell 10 acres of pines which the Forestry Commission had planted on the south-east corner of the wood in Lords Coppice. We sold the tops for Christmas trees and the trunks to make jumps for nutters on horses or to be pulped for the paper trade.

With the cash we realized, we were able to clear the ground, rabbit-proof-fence it and pay contractors to plant 30,000 Christmas trees. Now I sell large numbers for Christmas, plough all they earn into the 'Wood Account' and use it to pay for whatever needs doing on the reserve. If I want to hire a JCB digger to make an artificial badger sett, lay a drain, clear a ride or make a clearing, I do not count it as £200 or £300 but as a couple of hundred Christmas trees. It has made an enormous amount of difference to my scale of operations, because I can embark on projects we should have jibbed at if the cash had to flow from my pen.

Badgers have always been one of my major passions and I had already persuaded them to occupy two setts in the wood. The first was at Primrose Dell, where Michael Swales, chairman of the Staffordshire Wildlife Trust and head of the biology department of a well-known school, and his students helped soon after we arrived. The second – or House Sett – was behind a large rhododendron within 60 yards of the study window. Between the sett and the house are two wire-netted shelters, under which peanuts and flaked maize are concealed by heavy kitchen tiles. The shelters prevent deer taking the food before the badgers are around and the tiles stop squirrels or pheasant or wild duck entering through the pop hole and helping themselves. When the badgers arrive, they flick the tiles in all directions with their powerful fore feet – and trip a micro-switch, as they enter, which lights a small bulb which stands on the television. This allows us to switch the rubbish off, switch on a floodlight and sit back to watch the most enthralling 'live' entertainment of the night.

News of such eccentricity soon spread on the grapevine to other badger addicts and Charlie Parkes, the police sergeant in charge of rural crime, especially badger-digging, in Derbyshire, got in touch with me. He is a remarkable copper who has written extremely good books explaining the laws on trespass and poaching, firearms and rambling, conservation and pest control, hunting and coursing and egg collecting. He has also written the Countryside Rangers' handbook, *Law of the Countryside*.

Charlie and I had much in common, especially concerning badgers, because badger-digging in 'his' patch, which includes part of the Peak National Park, is particularly worrying. Gangs of urban thugs come out from Sheffield, Manchester and further afield with spades and terriers to dig out badgers, which they either bait with their own dogs or sell to be baited by other people. The going rate for a strong, freshly caught, wild badger is anything up to £500, and a fashion with drug barons and other major crooks is to invite their mates round on Sunday mornings for a few Scotches and a badger bait or an organized dog fight.

When Charlie contacted me he had just made a police training video, *Death of a Badger*, and he invited me to present and link it because of our common concern for this most persecuted of delightful and harmless creatures. His video drew heavily on video captured from a gang of baiters actually caught in the act. They started with a young badger in an enclosure from which it couldn't escape and 'entered' terriers to it. Several were put in together and they ripped and tore at their victim for a solid hour. The badger eventually became too weak to retaliate, so the baiters battered it to death with a fencing post. It was almost as cruel to the dogs, which suffered appalling injuries – the power of badgers' bites is notorious.

The spectators were so depraved that they had made a sixty-minute video, with graphic close-ups, of the whole obscene procedure so that they could 'enjoy' it all again and play back the most brutal parts. I am pretty hard-boiled but it made me feel physically sick and ashamed to belong to the same species as such louts.

Charlie's training video was most effective in showing policemen, who could scarcely believe such cruelty can exist in a supposedly civilized society, how vital it is to stamp out horror of this nature. The result is that he and his men have had considerable success in obtaining convictions against some of the culprits. But catching them in such wild, secluded countryside must always be partly by luck, even with the aid of radio communication and helicopters to follow their movements.

I decided to try to make some small contribution to badgers' safety by designing and constructing 'undiggable' artificial setts, or by making it harder to dig the animals out of their own setts, often excavated by generations of badgers. Purely by chance, the House Sett I had constructed in front of our windows fitted the bill.

When we had made the New Ride, pointing to the north east, we had cut up the trees we felled for fencing posts or logs and dug out the roots so that I could disc-harrow and cultivate a level ride before seeding and rolling it. We had bulldozed the tree roots – some very large – into a pile behind the rhododendrons, laid a couple of 10-inch-diameter pipes from the edge to the centre, below the roots, and covered the whole with tons of soil from the ditch bank. The result was a large pile of tree roots, with a tunnel entrance to their centre, covered by a mound of well-drained soil.

Nothing happened the first year – but then rabbits crept up the pipe to the centre of the mound and made comfortable couches beneath the roots, which kept them dry and warm. Later the foxes got in and dug out any 'easy' rabbit nests, leaving the fur and bedding of the nests outside the mound as evidence of their handiwork. Finally the badgers took to it and found it exactly to their liking. They have reared a litter of cubs there annually ever since and given us untold pleasure playing and feeding in the paddock in front of the window.

There would be nothing to stop diggers 'entering' a terrier to our sett (except me, if I caught them!), but, if they did, there would be no way of retrieving him, except waiting for him to come out. The badgers make their den – or 'overn' – under the largest, driest and warmest root piles. There is no way of getting at them from above without heavy mechanical equipment, powerful enough to extract huge roots. That would stand every chance of crushing both dog and badger as tons of trees and soil were shifted.

The general principle of creating an 'undiggable' sett is to construct it of roots, as we did, or with tree trunks or boulders which are too heavy to move by hand and piled too closely to allow access between them. Setts made by the badgers themselves can be equally well proofed simply by dragging or pushing large and heavy enough trunks and rocks over them to make it impossible to dig down to the tunnels by hand.

Gerald Springthorpe had considerable success with natural setts covered by rank grass or bracken. He first cleared the vegetation, being careful not to harm the roots. Then he scrounged old wire-netting fences which were decrepit enough to need replacement, and spread them, several layers thick, all over the area of the sett, cutting holes in the netting to coincide with sett entrances. He covered the netting with soil and, when the bracken or grass recovered, it pushed through the netting which became entangled with vegetation. Within a year it was quite impossible to pull away the netting, which was literally root-bound. Trying to dig through it was as fruitless as trying to dig through a spring mattress.

We have tried various other 'undiggable' setts in our reserve. By far the most ambitious had 12-inch-diameter spun-concrete pipes for its base. The pipes are made locally and damaged pipes, with broken flanges, can be had almost for the cartage. They weigh a third of a ton each, so need a JCB to handle them. We dug a trench in the bank above the pool in a sickle curve about 30 yards long, sloping gently down towards the pool so that any rain that did seep in, before the whole construction consolidated and weathered, drained out towards the pool and not back into the sett. We put 4 inches of broken stone 'chatter' in the bottom of the trench, which was about 3 feet deep, before rolling in the concrete pipes.

Instead of butting each pipe to the next, we left a 1-foot space between each pair and covered it with a paving slab so that, when badgers eventually took to it, they found a gap, 2 feet 6 inches below the surface, every 8 feet, from which they could excavate their own branch tunnels. We buried huge piles of tree roots near these exits – and covered the lot with good-draining, dry, friable soil, and seeded the top. Each entrance to the sett was carefully sited to be in unobstructed view of our sitting-room window, about 100 yards away, so that we could enjoy the fruits of our labour.

It was quite an expensive exercise, costing several hundred Christmas trees – but if I had been a keen gardener I dare say I might have lashed out a similar sum, once in a lifetime, to landscape a rockery or make a tennis lawn. Certainly no gardener or sportsman has derived more pleasure from his extravagance than we have. And, since I have not been away on holiday for twelve years or so, I do not have a guilty conscience.

We have made other – and cheaper – artificial setts in the wood. One was made of second-hand railway sleepers, nailed together with 6-inch nails to form inverted troughs and placed in trenches before back-filling. The troughs 'lead' to large, buried tree roots and it would be quite impossible to dig down to a terrier in this 'sett' – and remove three buried sleepers, nailed together – with shovels and grafting spades. Another equally successful sett was made from 10-inch diameter iron pipe, purchased as scrap when a local gravel pit was worked out. The pipe had directed water to clean the gravel, and it is just the size for badgers to crawl along.

Two years ago I had five artificial setts, all occupied by badgers which comprised two social groups using the wood, though none resided here before we came. Sadly, we have fewer badgers now, though the House Sett is still occupied and I saw five adults the night before writing this chapter. We do not know what happened to make our badger population decline, but they disappeared soon after young pheasants were put into local release pens. That may – or may not – be a coincidence, but it is common for modern syndicate shooters to 'control' foxes round their release pens with illicit, unselective poison and they are less skilled at it than old-time professional gamekeepers who could avoid harming badgers – if it was in their interest to do so. If hard evidence of this turns up, there are ways and means of discouraging the practice!

The benefits of dividing the wood into zones and managing each to provide a different habitat from neighbouring patches gradually emerged. Redstarts and long-tailed tits no longer passed through, but stopped to nest. In 1990 we had our first nesting pied fly-catcher. The limpid song of nuthatches, in summer, has become as common as their raids on suet and peanuts put out for the tits in winter. 'My' garden is a small wilderness in the bottom of the ha-ha with a rich harvest of teasels which attract 'seven-coloured linnets' (or gold-finches) in winter and a rich variety of butterflies on the purple flowers in summer. Woodcock, safe from shooters in the Christmas-tree patch in winter, reward us by staying to delight us with the hollow drumming of their wing feathers when they 'rode' round the rides in summer. Although the ground is heavy clay, slow-worms and lizards are occasionally to be seen. The sheer pleasure of creative work all over the reserve is sweeter than conventional riches.

But the most exceptional feature of the reserve is the unofficial partnership I have enjoyed with the Forestry Commission over the years. Bureaucratic departments are a little like hotels. They are as good or as bad as the current chef and manager, and it would be idle to pretend that we have not experienced ups and downs. Jack Chard, the conservator who pioneered an active concern for wildlife, was superb. His successor was not. John Fletcher, who followed, was as helpful as Chard and equally missed when he retired, and Gerald Springthorpe, upgraded from warrener by Chard, has been a close personal friend for years and was the thread of continuity till his health forced him to retire prematurely.

Soon after we bought Goat Lodge, a turkey tycoon purchased the adjacent estate and began clearing the ancient trees and 'other rubbish' to make prairies suitable for intensive arable farming. Deer in his crops were not calculated to be his flavour of the month. Our reserve had not then been fenced and formed a perfect sanctuary for local deer, and Gerald (rather against his will!) and I decided to cut down numbers far more drastically than necessary so as to give my new neighbour no reason for complaint. Gerald and a friend shot ten one morning, and considerably more later, and it was unanimously conceded that conservation – always a subjective concept – was a Good Thing!

Fallow deer are about the only subject on which Gerald and I do not see eye to eye. He has done so much for them and is so widely respected as an authority on them that it is natural for him to be firmly on their side, and his official job as head ranger entailed culling so many that the thought of killing them sickens him now.

The damage goats can do to any natural regeneration in woodland was brought home to me by the effect the Bagot goats had had on what was now our reserve, and I regard fallow deer almost as potentially harmful as goats! Where bottom cover is sparse, as it was in Holly Covert, deer nip off every young oak or beech or holly or bilberry which dares to show its head. They even bite off brambles until the stage is reached where briars and brambles are so rampant that they grow faster than the deer can eat them.

As with most things in the countryside, there is room for sensible compromise. We actually used deer as a management tool in the Christmas-tree patch by clearing the space and leaving it open for them to forage and kill regeneration for a whole season before planting the Christmas trees. It saved weeding for three years after planting, because the deer had eaten seedling trees – and there were no trees left to seed!

Our deer come up to the paddock and bird table to feed on grain I put out every evening and it interests us to see how many visitors, especially from towns, grow very excited when they see 'real' wild deer grazing fearlessly in the paddock and coming within 5 yards of the window to raid the bird table. All it really proves is how easy it is to manage wildlife by giving them a sense of security and food they love. Deer come as readily to feed on wheat as tits do for fat or badgers for peanuts if they have no reason to be afraid.

But deer are so beautiful and evocative that it is worth stretching a point over the damage they do to make them available, as an amenity, for the public to enjoy. Only by getting the public thoroughly on the side of those who wish to protect the countryside is it possible to hold out the danger of loss of votes for any political party which does not practise, as well as preach, protection of our rural heritage.

Gerald Springthorpe conceived the idea of persuading the Forestry Commission to do complementary management in Bagot's Wood, adjoining our reserve, where they hold a 999-year lease. John Fletcher, the conservator at the time, was cast in Jack Chard's mould, and so was his colleague, Norman Dannatt. They were anxious to co-operate – though there was no money in the kitty. But much of the softwood, planted thirty or forty years earlier, was coming up for thinning, roads were required for extraction which needed earth-moving equipment for construction, and the idea gradually blossomed.

There had been a marvellous colony of nightjars before the Military Valley was planted and an important ancient moss. Both were frost pockets and the young trees had not thrived, so it was not viable to replant them. It was not difficult to thin the softwoods selectively – a subjective term – so that the indigenous habitat of the ancient Forest of Needwood could be restored by natural regeneration. And the habitat which returned, more or less naturally, would be perfect as a staging ground for the surplus wildlife my management produced, attracting residents of its own to enrich the Forestry Commission's work.

The Nature Conservancy Council preaches the doctrine of creative conservation, but is not yet equipped to practise it because about the only legal protection it can provide is by designating Sites of Special Scientific Interest. And such sites are not designated until they already contain interesting species. The commission and I were a step ahead by *creating* sites which would attract and maintain interesting species, given reasonable time.

So the commission were unstinting with advice to help me succeed by doing, in our wood, precisely what they proposed to do in theirs. Our Christmas-tree patch, in Lords Coppice, already had superb stands of young oak and hornbeam, and mountain ash which was self-set and had regenerated naturally simply by being given light and space to grow and freedom from predation. It is a demonstration plot which shows what can be done in Bagot's Wood quite quickly. I was given advice on how much to allow contractors to thin my softwoods, leaving a 5-yard clearing round any young hardwoods which had survived and been 'drawn up' by the growing pines. The cash I got for the timber we felled will run the whole reserve for years and, the very first year after the pines were felled, bluebells and foxgloves burst through the mat of sterile pine needles on the forest floor.

We clear-felled the pines in just over 3 acres right in the centre of our wood and used the cash to fence it and pay contractors to plant it entirely with native, indigenous hardwoods, all of which bear food. The young trees were planted in grow-tubes to encourage rapid growth, and the take has been exceptionally good, despite the droughts in 1989 and 1990. In a few years the area will be a riot of wild crab apple and wild cherry, sweet chestnut and beech, wild servis and ash, with gorse and bramble and guelder rose as bottom cover. It will be a superb haven to conceal wildlife right in the heart of our wood and as far as possible from danger on the periphery. We shall be able to enjoy watching it, as it moves around or crosses boundary rides, through glasses from the window or from an observation tower on the edge of our New Plantation.

And finally Holly Covert, with its heronry, is a sample of what the commission's conservation area, which is indeed re-creative, will be in generations yet to come – perhaps with our heronry spilling over into it!

Jess and I were well pleased that the wildlife reserve we had spent half our married life creating had started on the right foot – and we had faith that it might prove to be the first link in a chain of such reserves where others would get equal satisfaction by emulating our habitat management all over the country in years to come.

SEVEN

THUNDERBOLT

The battle with CENTER PARCS

My study window is not only my favourite observation post from which to share the secrets of the wildlife in our wood; it also embraces wide skies to the south across the River Trent. This is the perfect arena for thunderstorms, which are doubly dramatic against the sombre backdrop of Cannock Chase, glowering back across the valley. Watching jagged blue tongues of forked lightning playing terminal tick across the sky is the perfect spectator sport. Seen from a distance of 5 miles, as the heron flies, it is remote enough to pose no danger. Countrymen believe that it never strikes twice in the same place and that thunderbolts can only strike the other man.

A particularly violent storm, high over the Vale of the Trent, did make me wonder, though! It gradually drifted in our direction, the interval between clap and flash steadily dwindling until, when it was directly overhead, it became impossible to detect the space between light and sound. As I watched, a simultaneous flash and violent explosion, just across the paddock, split a venerable great oak, from crown to roots, before my eyes. The dogs and I had stood there less than an hour before. It made my hackles rise, concentrating my mind on old wives' tales, because that storm, which began with a safety margin of several miles, had stalked us till it burst about our ears. Survival can sometimes be purely a matter of chance.

The analogy between my ambition to create a wildlife reserve, which

will be the first link in a national chain of similar reserves, and a storm-struck oak tree in the wood may seem pretty tenuous. But no chain is stronger than its weakest link and the weakest link in my chain is the possibility that outside forces, beyond my control, might destroy neighbouring habitat vital to the success of my life's work and the future potential for wildlife conservation in the area.

The first faint murmur of storms in the distance came when the man who owns the freehold of Bagot's Wood, immediately adjacent to Holly Covert, where our herons nest, remarked that he was thinking of selling his freehold so that his three boys would not be crippled by taxation when the Old Reaper mowed him down.

However trendy it may be to poke fun at large landowners and ancient county families for being paternalistic and feudal, the fact remains that they have been an impregnable bastion against exploiters of our rural heritage for centuries. Huge areas of precious English countryside have remained undefiled because a few powerful families, owning contiguous estates, have been doggedly determined to leave a heritage for their heirs as good as or better than their ancestors possessed. Having seen what death duties did to the estates of the Old Squire, the Squire and the Young Squire in my youth, I didn't blame anyone for stacking his chips out of reach of the taxman, if he could.

Within months of the publication of my book *My Wilderness in Bloom*, which described the creation and philosophy of our reserve, we began to hear distant rumbles which hammered home the dangers to our weakest link. Rumours on the grapevine, sowing seeds of doubt by forecasting obtrusive developments in Bagot's Wood, were difficult to pin down. At first they were as faint and innocuous as electrical storms on the horizon – too far away to pose any personal threat – but in spots as isolated as ours, everyone knows everyone else and strangers stick out like sore thumbs. So when woodmen spotted inter-lopers with maps and clipboards, suspicions were aroused. Smart city slickers, in posh cars we didn't recognize, sired speculation that the muck-and-Mercs mob had got their beady eyes on our neck of the woods. The story got around that Big Business planned a mammoth 'leisure complex' in the area – and the interval between clap and flash shrank as the menace of thunderstorms stalked us.

A conventional exercise in investigative journalism suggested that Center Parcs, then a Dutch developer, was planning to establish a leisure village in Bagot's Wood. I did not know what this was but soon discovered that it is newspeak for souped-up holiday camp, and that the first in this country had been established a year or so before in Sherwood Forest. I contacted the company's press office, asking for any sales promotional literature available without disclosing the reason for my interest. When it arrived, the distant thunderstorm beat it to the punch, filling the air with menace.

The sales guff which the postman brought described a 'leisure village' which would cost *£75 million*. It boasted of mod. cons. including permanent brick-built chalets, with central heating, telephone, television, fridge, jacuzzi bath and private balcony. A revolving French restaurant was promised, as were rapid tanners, Turkish baths, a gift shop and a fashion boutique. To top it off there would be computer-controlled lanes forming 'an exciting leisure bowl', which I gathered would make conventional sports activities seem as boring as real folk dancers on real village greens.

The *pièce de résistance* was a 'giant, transparent aquadome', maintained at a constant 84°F, with luxuriant displays of awe-inspiring tropical plants, bubbling jacuzzis, exciting water slides and a jungle river. A 'giant, transparent aquadome' leering over English woods or fields struck me as being as bizarre as a distended condom, symbolic of those who lust after the countryside for profit.

This 'leisure village' was to be built to accommodate no fewer than 300,000 happy holiday campers a year, who would go horse-riding through the wood, ride BMX bikes, play Robin Hood with bows and arrows, or simply 'luxuriate' in the semi-tropical giant aquadome. Since the kinkiest of my subliminal fetishes do not include being squeezed buttock to buttock with thousands of sweaty strangers, the brochure held no charms for me. The whole approach struck me as being either cynically misleading or, if written in good faith, as irresponsibly ignorant of the effect such incompatible intrusion would have on the environment and the wildlife which simply could not tolerate the resulting pressure.

One leaflet proclaimed that 'escape from the hustle and bustle of everyday life *back to the peace and tranquillity of nature is fundamental to Center Parcs* [my italics]'. It continued to extol 'the facilities of the village square under a giant transparent roof, which extends the sub-tropical experience'. Visitors were urged to take holidays in *specially created natural surroundings*'!

So far as specific plans for Bagot's Wood went, the company proposed to make a 25-acre 'artificial' lake and 3 miles of 'synthetic' streams in the Forestry Commission's creative conservation area, where they are re-creating the indigenous mixed woodland which once made

Needwood Forest one of the finest natural oakwoods in the country. This, Center Parcs assured us, would demonstrate their '*respect* for landscape, nature conservation and ecology'!! Their conviction was that they were 'at one with Nature'.

To commit what seemed to mc to be a mammoth act of environmental vandalism, they proposed to set on a gang of 800 construction workers for about fourteen months, carving their artificial lakes and synthetic streams and building their chalets. 800 construction workers would not normally be my first choice of labour grade to benefit wildlife or local residents! When they were gone, there would be no wildlife left to disturb, and the 300,000 jolly campers a year who would then move in would have written 'Finish' to any chance of wildlife – apart from paying campers – returning.

By this time the Forestry Commission, as leaseholder of Bagot's Wood, had been asked to disgorge the lease, which they would have to agree to do before Center Parcs could move in, even if the landowner, who still held the freehold, was anxious to sell. The commission had spent a considerable sum of taxpayers' money on making a conservation pool, which had been started by Gerald Springthorpe before his early retirement on health grounds. They had also begun large-scale selective thinning of softwoods, to allow the indigenous oaks and other hardwoods to thrive by natural regeneration as additional space and light were produced. The pines, which caused too much shade and canopy, were being selectively thinned. So, when they were asked to sell the lease, the commission quite rightly refused on the grounds that they were already combining a viable forestry enterprise with highly original and enlightened work on conservation of habitat for wildlife. The fact that they were combining with the experimental wildlife management which I had been carrying out next door for many years was also taken into consideration.

When he reached stalemate, the landowner 'broke the news' that he was going to sell his freehold to Center Parcs for a leisure village.

It was vital not to nudge things over the edge until I had been able to yell for help, so I played for time by stressing that such an incompatible intrusion so near to my reserve would make my wildlife management experiments unworkable. Instead of taking advantage of the natural reservoir from which my surplus wildlife could disperse naturally and gradually, all shy creatures would flee for their lives from so many human intruders.

He assured me that there would be no problems for my wildlife because Center Parcs' attitude to conservation was *far* more responsible than the Forestry Commission's. There would be no extra traffic along the drive, which divides our land, and campers would not come nearer than 25 metres from the drive boundary. The prospect of 300,000 jolly-makers, less than a cricket pitch away, did nothing for my confidence! I was not so optimistic so I continued to play for time by raising the question of an adequate 'buffer zone' between the holiday camp and me.

When I discussed the problems with knowledgeable friends, sometime later, they assured me that I was on a hiding to nothing. 'Money talks,' they said, 'and such money stinks. An ordinary chap like you stands *no* chance of stopping a £75 million speculative development.'

Not only had the second – and most violent – thunderstorm stalked me, but the thunderbolt had struck. Previous moonshine about lightning only striking the other chap floated like a ghost out of the window. The shattered oak was solid wood by comparison to me.

It was at this point, in my mid-seventies, that I suffered my second bout of worry guts, which had not afflicted me since the age of nine when my Mother died, leaving me feeling completely vulnerable. This time it affected Jess far worse than it affected me. Our wildlife reserve, for which we had worked so hard, meant everything to us and we could not bear the thought that it was in jeopardy. Knowing how much it means to me, Jess took the threat of disruption so much to heart that she couldn't sleep and felt really ill. I am much tougher – she says I am *too* hard! – and the effect on me was to make me so bloody-minded that I decided that, if this bolt from the blue really did shatter our reserve, I would pull away the pillars of the temple and bring damnation down on all concerned. It made me so one-track-minded and short-tempered that I became almost impossible to live with and it was the only episode in our fifty happy years that might have broken up our marriage.

The possibility of the total disruption of the character of the whole area of this important mixed woodland was so immediate and ominous that it filled our minds with, I believe, the same traumas experienced by the thousands who suffer unheralded – and unmerited – redundancy, hostile take-overs of the firms for which they work or financial catastrophe which makes repayment of the mortgage impossible. Our plight was as sinister as the sudden sack. Jess and I were submerged by the same bitter experience and stresses which drive victims back in search of rural living.

Perhaps describing the details of our campaign to defend our threatened patch may help others in a similar plight. It may be true that money talks and big money stinks – but big money does not always win and it is still true that a determined, ruthless, head-on attack will often encourage the opposition to back off. My Old Man's advice on dealing with bullies by punching them first, as hard as I could, on the nose has proved to be pretty sound.

While I was stalling for time I discovered just how devious minicrats and parish-pump politicians can get. The district council appeared hell-bent on getting the leisure village on their patch at all costs and they were taken aback when the Forestry Commission refused to sell the lease. The freehold itself had literally been worth nothing when the present owner had bought the estate, since it included no rights of management or ownership except the sporting rights, at a pep-percorn rent, until 1991. This effectively made it Crown property and local planners do not therefore have any jurisdiction over it. The only way to force the commission to give up possession was to persuade the Minister of Agriculture to compel the government to over-rule the commission's refusal to sell the lease.

To strengthen their hand, the council's head of public services issued a circular – at ratepayers' expense – to residents in the area which would be affected. This circular could not have put the case for a 'leisure village' more explicitly if Center Parcs had written the text themselves. But no space was made available for those who opposed such incompatible rural intrusion. So the parish council were forced to print and distribute their reasons for objecting without being sub-sidized, as the district council had been. The development would have transformed the whole character of the area.

The parish council voted unanimously against the project and Big Brother at the town hall received 151 written replies to his circular, of which 147 were against the holiday camp and only four in favour. The latter included the landowner, who wanted to sell, and his staff. Generous space was made available for him to air his case in the *official* report to the council, and this leaked report casually mentioned that the parish council was against the development.

By any standards a massive democratic thumbs down for the project had been demonstrated – but the district council treated it with what seemed like arrogant contempt by inviting Center Parcs to submit a planning application. In the event the company did not take up the invitation, but if they had, the council could have granted planning permission, against which there could have been no appeal short of persuading the minister to call the application in for a public enquiry. (There are provisions for 'objecting' if one's planning application is *refused*, but no provision for objectors to appeal against applications *granted*.)

Presumably Center Parcs decided not to apply because they were said to have agreed to pay the landowner a six-figure sum for the freehold when planning consent had been obtained. If the Forestry Commission had persisted in their refusal to sell the lease on the land where they had spent public funds on creative conservation, Center Parcs might have had to stump up hundreds of thousands of pounds for the freehold of land covered by planning consent – but still have been unable to gain possession because the tenant legally refused to quit.

The district council, apparently besotted with their desire for a prestigious but totally incompatible intrusion into precious habitat, produced a report to the planning committee recommending that Ivan Lawrence, the local MP, be briefed to take a delegation to the Minister of Agriculture to force the government to over-rule the Forestry Commission's refusal to sell the lease. The complete report was leaked to me, as are many such documents, because it is known that I do what I can to protect the environment from greedy exploitation which would rob future generations of their rural heritage.

The government had acted impeccably by allowing the Forestry Commission to honour their election pledge to protect the environment and this attempt by minicrats literally to over-rule the nationally elected government was typical of the petty officials who pander to the so-called enterprise society. If they had succeeded in forcing the government to over-rule the Forestry Commission, it would have opened the floodgates of demand for irreplaceable woodland nationally to be made available for speculative development. Future defence of precious sites by the commission would have been emasculated by the threat that the developer would get them over-ruled again if they demurred.

When I discovered that the council proposed to enlist the help of Ivan Lawrence, I wrote a few articles to try to clear the cobwebs. The council's leisure chief proudly proclaimed that 'tourism is a *business*, not just about pretty sites', adding that '*business* is about employment and creating great wealth for the area'. 'East Staffordshire,' he stated, 'suffers from an "*image crisis*" when selling itself as an employment location.' Gone are the days when responsible planners regarded protecting the environment for future generations as a sacred duty.

Jess and I have always counted our pennies and, though in no sense rich, we had put by £10,000 against a rainy day, perhaps to provide extra comfort should illness overtake us. We mulled over the threat to the environment and decided that we could think of no threat worse than to see our work going down the drain, so we put our money where our mouth was and offered £10,000 for the freehold of Bagot's Wood. I pointed out that the present rent brought in only £125 a year, and that the sum we offered, if invested, would produce ten times the present rent. I emphasised that I was not in the least interested in personal profit. All that I wished to ensure was that the priceless piece of varied woodland habitat where pressured wildlife flourished, because I had devised successful techniques to manage it, should never be put in peril again.

To make best use of our reserve it is vital to have the type of staging post the Forestry Commission's creative conservation area provided, from which 'my' surplus could disperse gradually and naturally. Far from profiting from this rare example of caring bureaucracy, all I wanted to do was to protect the result as a heritage for future generations. To do so, I also offered to donate the freehold of Bagot's Wood – if I could buy it – to the Staffordshire Wildlife Trust *before* the completion of the sale. This would ensure its protection for the future, because then there could be no 'change of use', except by compulsory purchase, without the consent of both the lessor and lessee. Even if the Forestry Commission were privatized in years to come, or there were a major change in government policy, the commission's conservation area would be sacrosanct if the Staffordshire Wildlife Trust owned the freehold. My offer was spurned.

So I publicized my feeling that a few parish pump politicians and petty officials on our local council were hell-bent on forcing central government to over-rule the Forestry Commission's refusal to sell the lease of Bagot's Wood.

If the commission's honourable resolve to uphold the election manifesto's promise to protect the environment could be defeated, the world would be the developers' oyster. Every government department which acted responsibly to defend our rural heritage in future would come under the threat of being dragged before the relevant minister, who would cut them down to size.

Then I received a surprise which went far to restore my faith in decency. Norman Tebbit, who also has a deep respect and affection for wildlife and the countryside, wrote to say that he had been distressed to see the threat to my reserve, but was happy to see reports in the *Daily Telegraph* that the problem had been solved. He said that he would have been prepared to take the matter up personally with the

Minister of Agriculture. In thanking him, I pointed out that I had merely won a reprieve, because Ivan Lawrence had been told by the council to lead a delegation to the minister to force the government to over-rule the Forestry Commission's refusal to sell the lease on the wood. So Mr Tebbit wrote to the minister about my reserve and the importance of the commission's work in Bagot's Wood. The minister replied that he felt that the commission were best placed to make their decision so that the case was not one in which he should intervene after they had done so.

Dr David Clark, Shadow Minister for Agriculture and Rural Affairs, had been extremely kind to me in the past by asking probing parliamentary questions which had been of great help in my efforts to reduce official extermination of badgers on the spurious charge that they were the vectors of bovine TB in cattle, instead of being no more than fellow victims. So I wrote to him to tell him of our plight, and he too sent a letter to the minister expressing his concern that Center Parcs were planning to establish a mammoth leisure park in Bagot's Wood, immediately adjacent to my reserve. He emphasized that 'if it were to be created on the scale envisaged, it would wreck his invaluable experiment'.

Living so close to the problem, it was difficult to see it in perspective, so we did what we have so often done when faced with problems needing sound, objective solution. We called for advice from an old and trusted friend. Patrick Cormack, FSA, MP, and his wife have been close friends for more than twenty years. He is at the spearhead of the heritage movement and shares our concern to leave the countryside in good shape for future generations and to guard it against harmful exploitation. He has an exceptionally wide circle of friends in Parliament, because concern for the countryside and national treasures falling into the broad category of 'heritage' are not constrained by party dogma.

The more widely it became known that the experimental wildlife management at Goat Lodge and the pioneering creative conservation by the Forestry Commission, which dovetailed with it, were threatened, the more distinguished and impartial politicians, of all shades of political opinion, jumped to the defence. The fact that politicians, of *all* parties, are prepared to sink political differences when the environment is threatened proved that, deep down, we have not yet all junked sanity for greed. John MacGregor, the Minister of Agriculture, heeded their pleas and stated categorically that the commission's decision not to sell the lease would stand and that development by Center Parcs would not go ahead. His successor, John Gummer, confirmed that his word was as good as John MacGregor's bond and he told me categorically that, 'The decision not to sell Bagot's Wood stands and I hope you are now fully reassured.' Richard Ryder, who moved to the Treasury, was equally specific.

A common ploy of bureaucrats who try to head off attempts to approach heads of departments or especially cabinet ministers, who could *order* them to accede to requests, is to maintain that it is middle rank bureaucrats who actually *frame* replies to voters' queries and that the Minister simply signs them, probably without seeing the details.

To substantiate this, I have collected several '*draft*' replies to questions I have raised, to which the reply from the Minister eventually conforms, word for word. Minicrats grow *very* twitchy if these are obtained because they know that they *must* have emanated as leaks from their own department!

A letter from John Gummer was therefore particularly interesting because it *proves* that *he* certainly reads replies to voters before they are sent, from the *hand written* postscript.

I had complained that the local shoot had been shooting wood pigeons, within 50 yards of my boundary, till lunchtime on *Easter Sunday*, apparently causing several sitting herons to desert. His postscript says, 'I am happy to say that Sunday shooting would be considered totally unacceptable in my own neck of the woods.' No subordinate member of his department would have written that, apart from the fact that it is in his own handwriting.

Another indication of the unselfish commitment to the environment of politicians at that level is the fact that he arranged for Dr Chris Cheeseman, the senior badger ecologist of the Ministry of Agriculture, to come to investigate when the badgers in my reserve dwindled catastrophically in numbers, soon after pheasants had been put into release pens by a local shoot. As mentioned earlier I suspected that the shoot were 'controlling' foxes and that, perhaps, my badgers were incidental victims.

I had campaigned for years against the Ministry's own policy of gassing and trapping badgers, which were alleged to be the vectors of bovine TB, undoubtedly causing the Ministry officials considerable trouble because of the adverse publicity. So I really did appreciate John Gummer's generosity in sending his top scientist to advise on *my* troubles! It was impossible to *prove* the cause of decline, though his advice hardened my suspicions.

Companies willing to invest £75 million on such development are not easily deflected. Although I was told that they would not come nearer than 25 metres from the edge of the drive, it did nothing to mollify me, so Clive Gordon, the Director of Development for Center Parcs, came for lunch to step up the bidding.

Before he came, I did my home work and gathered that Mr Gordon had wide experience in such matters. He had been the Assistant Director of Countryside for Nottingham County Council and worked in close harmony with Andy Stewart, MP for Sherwood, during negotiations for planning consent for Center Parcs' first 'leisure village' in Sherwood Forest. When planning consent had been accomplished, I was told that Mr Gordon left the employment of the County Council to become Director of Development for Center Parcs.

Andy Stewart, as Parliamentary Private Secretary to the Minister of Agriculture, seems to have been a potentially useful ally.

Mr Gordon stressed that Center Parcs would leave a buffer zone, of undisclosed size, between their 'leisure village' and my reserve; and, when he wrote to confirm the meeting, he suggested managing it with a trust, to be appointed by the developers. This, in practice, would obviously give the trustees complete power to vary the size and conditions of the buffer zone, so I declined with thanks.

The Council were pressing them to apply for planning permission but, if they had complied and purchased the freehold of the wood, the Forestry Commission still held the leasehold which gave them *full* management control, so that acquisition of the freehold could still fail to get possession.

They appear to have calculated that, if I withdrew my opposition, the five politicians of Cabinet rank who had, by this time, interceded with the minister, would withdraw. The Forestry Commission's refusal to sell the freehold could then be over-ruled. So an emissary arrived at my house, on a Saturday morning, with an offer to arrange a buffer zone of 200 acres between my reserve and the 'leisure village'. I was told that this zone would be in my sole, legal ownership, and that the drive between the buffer zone and my wood would be closed and a new access made to the landowner's farm through the wood. This would enable me to make the 200-acre buffer zone and my 90-acre wood one complete wildlife reserve to be managed solely by me by any method I chose.

The offer of 200 acres, in my unconditional ownership, was very tempting. Immediately next to my reserve, it would have been enough to protect the conservation work I had done for the foreseeable future. But my acceptance would have kicked the ground from under the

Forestry Commission's feet, because the powerful political backing they had received against sale of their 999-year lease had been based on the fact that intrusion into their conservation area would jeopardize my work in what is acknowledged to be a reserve of national importance, and their own creative conservation dovetailed with it. If the commission's refusal to sell their lease had been over-ruled on the grounds that a buffer zone I accepted gave me all the protection I needed, the commission would have been defenceless, not only here but all over the country. Any future resistance they raised could have been silenced by the threat that, if they did not co-operate, the developer or planners would get them over-ruled again.

On top of this, our parish council had leaped 100 per cent to the defence of my reserve and, if they had been defeated, 300,000 holiday campers on their doorstep would have destroyed the character of the whole area. So I turned the offer down.

News of my stand got around and I was approached by the Cotswold Water Parks Village Society, who sought my help because a competitor of Center Parcs was trying to obtain planning consent for a 'holiday town' on similar lines to the 'leisure village' we were fending off. This was to be the size of Lockerbie, between four small villages whose combined size and population were less than that of the development threatened, so it would obviously destroy the rural character of the whole area. The society sought my support because they felt that various bodies who had originally opposed the project had been too easily reassured by grand sounding promises, just as the attempt seems to have been made to silence me by the offer of a substantial buffer zone. Much as I would have liked to help, I replied that I was more than fully occupied defending my own reserve, but I promised to do whatever I could if the opportunity arose.

I spoke prophetically! Within a couple of weeks a stranger phoned, saying that he worked for a public relations agency and that he had been briefed to see if I would be willing to act as an environmental consultant for a client who wished to establish *six* leisure developments in this country and, possibly, some on the continent. I had no intention of obliging, but decided that it was well worth investigating to see what made such ventures tick.

As the first step in the game of hard-to-get, I said I was too busy but, if he was still interested, I asked him to try later. 'How much later?' he asked. I told him to give it a month and he said that that was fine as they might require me as an expert witness at a public enquiry, due to be heard in the autumn, about a project at the Cotswold

Water Parks. The sheer coincidence was a compelling reason to follow the matter up.

I therefore phoned the organization which had asked for help and told them that, if they heard strange rumours that I had ratted on them, they should not worry. I would keep them abreast of developments.

Continuing the game of hard-to-get, I said that the only time I had free was a Saturday morning, at my house. Max Pearce, the managing director of Lakewoods, the leisure subsidiary of Granada, arrived with two henchmen in a trendy Range Rover. They spent the next two hours seeking my services as environmental consultant, but insisted that I name my own terms. I made it clear that I would need to know a great deal more about them and their proposals before agreeing on *any* terms. But, *if* I agreed, I should require £1000 a day plus VAT and expenses, and I asked how many days they envisaged they would require my services. They made no objection to the proposed terms of £1000 etc. and said I should set aside 100 days. We were talking about a hundred grand!

The man from Granada had two witnesses. I had none, so I recorded what had been said, in writing, as soon as he left, and asked him to confirm the terms offered. He replied by return, repeating his invitation, asking how I wished to approach the assignment and the fee arrangement required!

I told him that I am so committed to conservation interests that I should say 'No' so often that he would not get value for money, and that if there were any bad apples in the barrel, in the form of 'bent' boffins or disaffected bureaucrats, respectable consultants would be tarred with the same brush, however innocent they were. Having spent my life forging what I believe to be an impeccable reputation, I said that I was not prepared to take the slightest risk of being lumped with those who might find it expedient to 'edit' the facts to suit the interest of their clients. Where fees of £1000 or so *a day* are so far out of phase with what consultants earn as specialists in conventional fields, the temptations are obvious and none the less because they may be subconscious.

He wrote to say how sorry he was that I felt unable to take up his offer but that he 'respected my view that, as a champion of conservation interests, I felt it important to preserve my independence'.

I have no reason to doubt the integrity of this prospective client, because I formed the opinion that he was not only honest but shrewd enough to cash in on less upright competitors by deliberately setting out to provide 'leisure developments' which were 'environmentally friendly'. If he could achieve a reputation for being on the side of the angels, he would obviously have the edge over rivals who might use more unscrupulous means to get planning consent for incompatible rural developments – and good luck to him for preparing the wolves for slaughter. But what a commentary on 'the system' if such tactics are accepted as being necessary to outflank unscrupulous developers and petty officials!

Since the district council had canvassed local opinion about the proposed holiday camp in the priceless mixed woodland next to me – and treated the response with contempt – I told Ivan Lawrence, our local MP, about the offer. His party manifesto had specifically included promises to protect the environment against exploitation, so I assumed he would leap into the fray in support of his constituents whose wishes, in my opinion, had been cynically flaunted.

He replied that he 'wondered if any other of his constituents could have resisted the temptation'! Knowing plenty of honest men who would not sell their integrity for a few pieces of silver, I told him that I thought he under-rated his constituents, suggesting that he was perhaps measuring them by more elastic political yardsticks.

Thoroughly disillusioned to discover that it appears to be so widely accepted that 'every man has his price' and that there really *are* 'offers which can't be refused', I passed the whole file over to the *Daily Telegraph* – which allotted a quarter-page for me to highlight the matter in an article entitled 'The Price Nature Pays for Advice'.

I cashed in on my unexpected dalliance with the opposite camp by enquiring what steps they would have taken if the Forestry Commission had continued to stall development by refusing to disgorge their 999-year lease. One possibility, I gathered, would have been to negotiate for renewal of the sporting lease, at almost *any* price, when it fell in, as the lease on Bagot's Wood was due to do in two years' time.

The commission's policy is to consider the interests of sport, amenity and conservation, and they are punctilious about avoiding giving offence to landowners by appearing to be anti-sport. Hunting and shooting are almost invincible policital lobbies. But if it could subsequently be shown that the commission had spent public funds creating a wildlife conservation area – and then cashed in by letting the rights to shoot the wildlife they conserved, it would be very difficult for them to contest a planning application for almost any other activity which was demonstrably less incompatible with wildlife conservation than shooting the wildlife conserved!

On the banks of the commission's conservation pool in the wood were drums of grain, put there by the shoot to feed the duck and to seduce them to come within range of guns waiting to shoot them. This was perfectly legal within the terms of the existing sporting lease, if possibly anti-social. But it raised the question of whether it was more than a coincidence that the council had dropped broad hints in their draft structure plan that proposals for leisure development in Bagot's Wood would be welcome.

Since the Forestry Commission is classed as Crown property, immune even from *consideration* of development proposals by planners without prior Crown consent, it seemed somewhat presumptuous of the council to canvas for proposals, to put it at its kindest. I imagine the commission were less than pleased.

The countryside could so easily become no more than a political pawn to catch votes by promising everyone everything – and then allowing bureaucrats and councillors to cash in by putting the development rights up for auction.

The Forestry Commission was hammered unmercifully – and often rightly! – for years because of its callous treatment of wildlife, and nobody spoke his mind more ruthlessly than I did over shooting deer with shotguns, snaring badgers and shooting foxes – or deer – with lights at night, when it may be impossible to find the wounded and put them out of their misery.

But as an objective countryman, with first-hand experience, I know of no government body that has changed more and yet got no credit for sticking to its principles against determined opposition. The commission's stand against big business in refusing to disgorge the lease on Bagot's Wood, because of the conservation work they are doing there and because it is an example of invaluable, native mixed woodland, was an impeccable example of honouring central government's pledge to protect the environment.

Yet there are moves afoot to make the Forestry Commission responsible to local planning authorities, ostensibly to prevent them from smothering the landscape with sterile foreign pines.

It is the supreme example of the pot calling the kettle black, because the respected planners, who once regarded it as their sacred duty to protect the countryside against exploitation, have too often been replaced by miserable minicrats who help rich developers grow richer.

By practising what many more conservationists preach, the commission is demonstrating that there is yet a chance to leave at least part of the English countryside unspoiled which would otherwise have been a cheapjack 'theme park' or holiday camp, where a rash of timeshare shacks could be all that was left for the future.

It will not be easy, though. The chairman of the Forestry Commission told me that in letting sporting rights to landowners he took into consideration 'conservation, recreation, and amenity interests, as well as operational requirements'! It would be difficult to choose areas of greater potential conflict, either politically or physically, and every credit is due to the commission for having the courage to cope with such differing needs.

There are those who believe that, just as fresh air is the right of all, so is access to the countryside, especially moorland and forests. The fact that most heather moorland owes its continued existence to the sport of grouse-shooting is conveniently ignored, because those who believe they should be able to romp at will on wild moors are often the same people who think shooting for sport is immoral and should be stopped. If it *were* stopped, and heather were no longer managed, as it has to be to provide correct breeding and feeding habitat for grouse, the moors would degenerate to scrub and end by being swathed in commercial softwoods which would spoil the view.

But the grouse-shooters are not whiter than white and, when they rent or own the moors, some think it is their inalienable right to exterminate anything which interferes with their sport, including pressured raptors or predatory birds of prey and, of these, hen harriers especially. Such an attitude, not surprisingly, puts the ornithologists in orbit! As raptors were around before rich sportsmen, they might think that they too have 'rights' to a few grouse, which formed part of their natural prey before currency was invented.

It is widely accepted that the sheer pressure of visitors is destroying parts of footpaths in our National Parks and that it has been necessary to pave them with unsightly concrete. Far less pressure on the 'amenities' of woodland is needed to cause comparable damage, because the mere presence of people drives away shy birds and timid deer. If the intruders include uncontrolled dogs, the damage can be terminal. However, birds and beasts don't vote, so the minicrats resent giving either funds or protection to *any* habitat, however sensitive, if Johnny Voter can't get in to 'enjoy' it. The purpose of my reserve is to create a reservoir of wildlife – which can live a full life in our wood because we provide it with ideal conditions and the indispensable sense of security. I see nothing wrong with that, but there are those who believe it is unjustified either to spend public funds or to give planning protection to land where the public does not have freedom to do whatever it likes.

In trying to strike a realistic balance the Forestry Commission therefore walks a tightrope from which there is always someone hell-bent on tipping them – and more power to their elbow for setting an example of constructive conservation. The remedy they seek is to try to zone activities so that they are far enough apart not to conflict. Large patches of dense conifers, which support little wildlife because the dark, sterile understorey grows little vegetation, and where there are few houses or none at all, can tolerate holiday camps and funfairs and orienteers because there is nothing and nobody for them to disrupt. Natural, mixed hardwoods, which take centuries to grow, compared to mere decades for softwoods, are quite obviously too precious to be sacrificed lightly.

Properly conducted shooting can be tolerated by creatures which are not excessively shy, but some modern syndicate shoots are little more than status symbols for people who are not knowledgeable enough to understand what is acceptable by wildlife and what is not. Many such shoots do as much harm to predators, such as hawks and owls and badgers, through ignorance, as old-fashioned gamekeepers did with callous disregard.

'Green' issues are in the ascendant, so the commission can afford to err more on the side of compassion now than it could in the past. The intelligent public is likely to be more critical of disruptive behaviour towards wildlife by commission tenants, and more supportive of civilized behaviour, which draws the fire of the huntin', shootin' and fishin' set, than at any time in the past.

It is up to responsible people to give active backing to the Forestry Commission's efforts.

EIGHT

THE CATALYST

Several months after publication in the *Daily Telegraph* of my article 'The Price Nature Pays for Advice', I received a letter from a perfect stranger, a Dr Coles, who announced the intention of forming an Institute of Environmental Assessment, which was to be 'a professional institute to create standards and to police professional activities amongst environmental consultants'. My experience in being offered fees so high as to pose temptation to give biased advice, however honourable the prospective client, is not, of course, unique.

Dr Coles said that the institute was to be inaugurated at the House of Commons and that he would be grateful if I would assist at the official launch, 'since your article acted as a catalyst for many of the ideas'. The chemistry I learned at school could easily be contained in the bottom of a test tube, but I did remember that a catalyst produces chemical reactions without undergoing permanent change itself.

I have always regarded my experimental work on wildlife management as being a personal but totally insignificant contribution to providing habitat which would benefit wildlife in the future. It had surprised and, I confess, delighted me to discover how willing distinguished politicians had been to come to the rescue when I cried for help. I was even more delighted that scientists – whom I often criticize for being too specialist and academic – should discover that my abrasive views might be a catalyst or spark to light the flame, which might cauterize abuse. I had no way of knowing whether Dr Coles and his friends would turn out to be boring boffins, simply blinding each other with science, or whether they might prove to be a dynamic force, capable of exposing bureaucratic malpractice. But humble backwoodsman like me are not often invited to speak to meetings in the House of Commons, so I accepted his invitation with alacrity.

When confirmation came I discovered that I was to be one of four speakers. Conal Gregory, MP for York, was the sponsoring MP. Dr Coles was to describe the functions and purpose of the new institute. I was invited to explain the possible value of such assessment and policing of consultants for conservation, and Lord Nathan would assess the way forward.

During my train journey to London, a stranger at the same table told me, out of the blue, that he had enjoyed the television programme, One Man and his Dog, which had been transmitted the previous night. Then emerged the real reason for his introduction: curiosity.

'And what are you doing, going up to the big city?' he asked. 'You can't be sheep dogging up there?'

A hazard – and sometimes pleasure – of being on the box is that perfect strangers often accost you under the impression that you know them as well as they feel they know you after seeing you regularly in their sitting-room. It is most encouraging – and useful – if they like the programme, to discover precisely why they do so. It may then be possible to sharpen the angles of presentation which are obviously probing home. It is equally useful to discover what falls flat – those who are not hard-faced enough to thrive on criticism should choose a gentler art.

I discussed precisely what aspects of the previous night's broadcast had given my travelling companion pleasure and then earned my keep by telling him where I was going and why I'd been asked.

'You're on a loser, mate,' he said. 'You can't beat the power of big money – or the way it is misused.'

He went on to say that, by coincidence, he was a professional consultant himself. His line of business was not conservation but civil engineering. He was employed to give advice on the alternative routes for roads, either as bypasses or major routes between cities.

When a new road was required, there were always a number of different routes it could follow, each of which had to be surveyed. Some would be physically easier (and cheaper) than others because the terrain was either more suitable or more difficult because of gradient or soil, open spaces or trees or buildings. Some would cause hassles because they would ruin amenities of villages or beautiful countryside; others might destroy the habitat of rare species or damage Sites of Special Scientific Interest. The permutations were infinite and relative merits often purely subjective so that the consultant usually had the choice of several solutions to put forward. Here was the rub.

His fee, based on the time the investigation took and its complexity could vary enormously. So it was in his interest – and that of his employer – that his recommendation should be as expensive as possible. This obviously suited the company appointed to carry out the job, since their profit would be a percentage of the final cost. The bureaucrats who would issue the planning consent would expect the contractor to cover the cost of supplying islands or bridges crossing existing roads or to replace buildings which had to be demolished with something better (known in bureaucratic circles as 'planning gain'). Arguments among parish-pump politicians can often be swayed by the fact that this or that route, which might be socially objectionable, would be more than compensated for by a splendid new community centre or other prestigious edifice that would 'dignify' the district.

Only those who believe in Santa Claus could be conned into swallowing the story that planning gain comes out of developers' own pockets. The obvious way to provide such largesse for the community is to inflate the initial quotation to cover it. Obviously a percentage of the inflated price would be included in legitimate developers' profits – so everyone was happy. If the developer also happens to be an apple which has been in the barrel too long, he may be very compliant. Giving 'sweeteners' or back-handers as the price of signing a contact may escalate the price (and likewise the profit) further. The bigger the cost, the more 'prestigious' the development, and even many honest bureaucrats are extremely susceptible to the resulting prestige.

My travelling companion, the civil engineering consultant, opened my eyes to possibilities of spiralling costs caused either by dishonest greed or deplorable hankering after status-symbol 'prestige'. But he also shook my faith in my chances of helping the Institute of Environmental Assessment to make the slightest dent in the graft which seems to be rotting the guts of practices which Dr Coles proclaimed need his institute to 'create standards and police professional activities among environmental consultants'.

Arriving, daunted, at the House of Commons, I was ushered past police checkpoint after checkpoint into the bowels of the building. Judging by the standard of security, villains were expected in every corridor, though they were presumably more likely to be disciples of Guy Fawkes than financial fiddlers. I decided, when my turn came to take the stage, that I would jump in and make a splash which would ensure that my visit was not forgotten.

Lord Nathan, who introduced me, was very flattering, which bolstered my self-confidence. It was encouraging to discover that an unknown naturalist, who had enjoyed a quarter of a century's idyllic work with creatures he loved, in the obscurity of his wood at the back of beyond, should be invited to lob a few bricks at the bureaucratic malpractices he despised. So I rose to the occasion and pulled no punches.

Apparently the fee I had been offered was about par for course, but I suggested that a priority for the new institute should be to force disclosure of all fees so that voters could see for themselves where great temptation to stray from the straight and narrow path of rectitude lay.

I highlighted the weakness of Sites of Special Scientific Interest, which are often so specialist and academic that what is of special interest to scientists may seem totally irrelevant to normal folk. Such boffins may grow so obsessed with chasing rarity that they catch only obscurity. I suggested that, instead of pandering to such eccentrics, the Nature Conservancy Council would do better to take active steps to encourage *creative* conservation, to produce and manage habitat which would ensure the survival of creatures we take for granted today which will be rare – or extinct – in a few decades if we take no steps to provide for their needs.

The crested newts of my youth now need legal protection to survive. The time to encourage people to erect bird or bat boxes is *when* they put them up. Waiting till they have been tenanted by some obscurity which might be of 'special' interest only to scientists may well be too late.

There were about a hundred politicians, big businessmen and scientists at the meeting in the Commons and, when questions subsided, we mingled over drinks and sandwiches. I was approached by a man who sympathized with my sentiments but echoed the doubts of my fellow traveller on the train.

Our enterprise society was only interested, he said, 'in making profit.

The more a job costs – the greater the profit from a fixed percentage.' His job, it seemed, was producing chemical treatment for sewage effluent. When this was passed through the system he was trying to sell, it was so pure that it was fit for drinking – better, I gathered, than the fluid which flows from London taps, which is said to have passed through half a dozen Cockneys and been returned to the river before being decanted in hotel bedrooms for visitors' morning cuppas.

Yet my informant was on the breadline, because the apparatus his company expected him to sell was not uncompetitively expensive: it was too cheap! Competitors could send untreated sewage out to sea where it did untold harm to the environment. It was several times the cost of the chemical treatment, but consultants advising on alternatives wrote his system off because their cut of the gross profit would have been less. Unless the new Institute of Environmental Assessment could persuade politicians to expose the rot and cure it – which he doubted – tycoonery would triumph every time.

If such allegations are really true – and I believe they are – it would be difficult to envisage a more inflationary malpractice, and the cost of living will continue to spiral until such sabotage is exposed and the perpetrators are ostracized.

Never having dabbled in politics until forced to defend my own life's work, I have found such encounters pretty daunting, so I made a reconnaissance of the opposition to establish some strategy of defence.

The consultant on the train and the chap who dealt with sewage effluent were in no minority of folk of a like mind. The fact that I have been pretty outspoken about human parasites of the environment has prompted some surprising leaks of normally confidential information.

Cases of officers resigning from public service to set up as consultants seem fairly common. An irate correspondent described how her local officer, heavily subsidized from her taxes, took a golden handshake to retire early – and then appeared as a 'consultant' in the same area. His deputy was promoted to his job – it was said that the two of them would be a useful combination! – but was then jacked up even higher, on a short-list of one, and against some opposition. The chief beneficiaries, my correspondent alleged, were developers and those to whom they passed sweeteners.

Such stories are difficult to substantiate and might be risky to expose because of our draconian laws of libel. *Private Eye* magazine prints a regular column, 'Rotton Boroughs', about such cases, and occasionally lands in court as a result, but damages for libel seem to be taken as part of the overheads by such periodicals. Several cases of alleged unethical conduct in my own district council are currently being investigated by the local ombudsman but, judging by previous form, I do not expect a conclusive result.

I was approached myself by a reputable scientist I had known for years who said he had just been made redundant as a result of government spending cuts. He had set up as an independent planning consultant and his first assignment involved a development which would involve moving a colony of badgers so that his clients could build over the sett. This would require a special licence from the Nature Conservancy Council. Knowing my involvement in the protection of badgers, he was phoning me to ask if he could give my name as a reference. I told him that I was more interested in the welfare of badgers than boffins. I have no reason at all to doubt his integrity, but if the consultancy fee he had been offered was comparable to the £1000 a day I was offered by Lakewoods – and if his sudden arrival on the labour market happened to coincide with high mortgage repayments or other liabilities – the temptation to be more sympathetic to his employer's interests than to the welfare of the badgers would have been great.

Another man I knew as ex-director of the Royal Society for Nature Conservation turned up as consultant for the prospective developer of the Cotswold Water Parks. Like the scientist who wanted me to vouch for him in his recommendation to move a colony of badgers for a building development, he was, so far as I knew, above suspicion.

But both were so distinguished in their scientific or conservation fields that the inspector at a public enquiry would have been likely to take their word as gospel against the most impassioned – and possibly more objective – protestations from the local naturalists' trust or other concerned enthusiasts with deeper local knowledge.

My informant at the Institute of Environmental Assessment told me that any consultant who provided advice which did not fall in with his client's wishes would be unlikely to be commissioned for many encores!

About a hundred people, concerned in one way or another with the future of the environment, had turned up at the first meeting of the Institute of Environmental Assessment to see whether such an independent organisation had any chance of success. Policing and improving the quality of advice available to help local authorities and developers not to be biased in favour of whoever employs the consultants is very necessary. Some industrialists were prepared to fund the institute until it was financially self-supporting, if the prospect was good. Politicians were there to see what votes were in it for them. Press and scientists were there to decide which side of the fence had the more promising landing, or which angle made the most compelling story.

The disturbing thing is that when the media get potentially explosive leads, they tend to shrug them off, observing cynically that 'we all know politics and local government are rotten and corrupt. There is no news story there.' This is partly because it is very difficult to get hard, incontrovertible facts and figures; but when I was able to supply solid evidence of my own experience – the whole correspondence leading up to my offer of four-figure fees – I was given the space to expose the risk I saw.

Making the point that it is the (possibly) exceptional bad apples in the barrel who need controlling, I focused on types who become successful millionaire developers. Those who fall by the wayside don't make news. The sort who hit the headlines often start in the gutter and make their pile in a very few years. Scrappies, starting with a handcart and loud voice, trade in government surplus or buy derelict land for peanuts and flog it for development. Conventional strippers are ladies of easy virtue who sell their charms to stiffen the flagging pride of seedy old men – but at least it is their own charms they sell. Their modern counterparts are the spiv developers who asset-strip the heritage of future generations.

To notch up £1 million within a few years needs a lot of luck and judgement – or total lack of scruples; often all three. Such successful entrepreneurs star regularly in local papers, all over the country, under thin veils of innuendo which whet the appetites of those who can read between the lines. Sadly, such speculators rarely rest on their laurels and sit back to plough some of their lucky lolly back into the environment which they exploited to acquire it. Their ambition is to make another £1 million – and another and another, until they reach the Top Two Hundred Richest Men. Then their dominant greed spurs them on to reach the Top Hundred and Fifty and the Top Hundred.

Greed and graft are not the only dangers to the future of the countryside. When publicity about the prospects of work on my own wildlife reserve escalated, an MP turned up to examine it for himself. He also 'wondered if any of his other constituents could have resisted the temptation' of a very high fee to join another camp. When I had shown him around, he asked to see the creative conservation being carried out by the Forestry Commission, immediately adjoining our reserve, which is so important as a staging ground for the surplus wildlife my management produces.

Although I enjoyed the most cordial relations with the commission, I would have considered it the height of bad manners to take anyone else – especially an MP – on their property without specific permission, but he said that, if he was to back my stand, it was important that he saw it. He had called on a Saturday afternoon, when commission staff were off duty, so I phoned Gerald Springthorpe at home, and asked him to come over right away. As already explained, it was Gerald who had conceived the management plan in the wood next door. He had devoted the whole of his working life to improving the commission's image for conservation, and I was sure there could be no objection to the work being explained by him. Gerald simply exudes enthusiasm about his pet subject, on which he is deeply respected, not only by those who care about our countryside here, but on the continent as well.

The conducted tour was in full swing when we came to the large pool he had made by damming a valley; it was the true pride of his life.

'Look at this pool,' he said. 'It was dry land two years ago. Now it contains crested newts.' To have persuaded species, under enough pressure to require special legal protection, to move in so soon and breed, was *real* triumph, in his eyes, and in mine as well.

There was an awkward silence as our guest groped for a suitable comment. 'Crested newts,' he said, 'crested newts – they turn into frogs, don't they?'

Slow on the uptake, I looked at him, unable to decide whether he really thought newts turned into frogs or if he had an unsuspected, wry sense of humour and was gently pulling our legs. I had no chance to test either theory because Gerald simply fizzed into orbit, spitting out his contempt for urban politicians.

'Newts turn into frogs?' he hissed. 'You an MP, responsible for protecting the future of the countryside, and you think newts turn into frogs?'

There was no further opportunity to discover whether the remark had been made in jest or conviction, because our guide never drew breath for long enough to leave room for a reply.

I dined out on the episode for weeks – but it was symbolic of the magnitude of the task which confronts those who really care about the countryside. Whether it was misplaced humour or ignorance, it was a yardstick of the gulf between our urbanized society and those of us who will really care if the countryside is sacrificed for short-term gain. Ignorance, in policy-making circles, can be as damaging as greed at grass roots. There are those who think neither is funny.

The quality of any organization can swing from superb to rotten in phase with the performance of the people running it. Even the Forestry Commission, for whom I normally have the highest respect, has given me some nasty jolts. Two of the conservators responsible for our area of the country have been committed conservationists, the one 'finding' and building up Springthorpe and the other delegating responsibility to him which put Cannock Chase and Bagot's Wood among the pioneers of creative conservation. A third conservator, wedded to the concept that trees were only for profit, appeared to resent the publicity which was focused on innovative work for wildlife, and so cut the corns of wildlife officers and rangers.

One head ranger, recruited to the latter type of regime, put wildlife low among priorities and resented my complaint that badgers seemed to be decreasing in his neck of the woods. He said that there were plenty of badgers, as many as there had ever been. To rub my nose in how little amateurs like me know about badgers, he pointed to a well-worn track through a gap in the fence near which we were standing. 'There,' he said, 'look at *that* track. It is obviously well used,' and he stooped to pluck the tuft of hair off a bramble at the edge of the fence. He waved it under my nose in triumph and challenged me to deny that the track was a veritable badger main road. Unfortunately for him, the tuft of hair was brown and more silky than a badger's. It had been left on the thorns from the coat of a muntjac deer, which is small enough to use gaps in fences no larger than would be required by badgers or foxes or hares! It underlined the need for selecting staff on the ground who have no need to bluff because their competence is unquestioned.

Intensive agriculture is certainly among the other major problems to be tamed because, in spite of the crippling cost of financing surplus food mountains in the European Community, the agro-chemical industry seduces farmers to buy more and more chemicals to produce higher mountains of corn, deeper lakes of milk and ever more sticky bogs of butter. Unwanted straw is burned off and the roots ploughed in to produce a harvest of slugs next year to rival this year's corn harvest. So the agro-chemical wide-boys flog tons of metaldehyde slug pellets to kill the slugs.

The Ministry of Agriculture carried out a post mortem on a heron from our reserve and confirmed death by metaldehyde poisoning –

which is claimed to be the first case diagnosed in a heron! It was ever likely to be because they had never tested for metaldehyde till I prodded them. If it kills the herons that eat the frogs that eat the slugs, it will kill other species of birds and badgers and hedgehogs. But irresponsible big business doesn't want to know about anything which might nibble into its profits.

We had a nice lot of hares on the reserve twenty years ago, but they have disappeared. Since hares also nibble into profits, they are classed as vermin, so nobody cares about them. But they were natives for centuries before William the Conqueror introduced rabbits, so perhaps their 'right' to continued existence here is really as great as ours.

In her pioneering book, *Silent Spring*, Rachel Carson alerted us to the horrors of some of the worst poisons spewed over the fields in the name of efficient 'control' of pests and weeds, fungi and other pilferers of profit. But even her powerful message could not conquer the greed which cares nothing for what is obliterated so long as there is profit on the bottom line. Aldrin, dieldrin and heptachlor were the chlorinated hydro-carbons which exterminated hundreds of thousands of birds that ate seed-corn dressed with insecticide. They killed again when predators ate the dying birds and scavengers ate the predators. The chain of destruction was horrific and public outrage at Rachel Carson's disclosures curbed the worst of the excesses.

For some years the Ministry of Agriculture issued an annual booklet entitled *Approved Products for Farmers and Growers*. 'Look before you buy,' it advised. As a book for bedside reading, it was guaranteed to induce horrific nightmares, because it listed the chemicals available for pest and weed destruction, along with the necessary precautions to be taken.

One soil-acting herbicide, for example, had to be incorporated to a depth of at least $1\frac{1}{2}$ inches within *30 minutes* of spraying and no land treated could be planted with any crop but brassicas for *4 months* after spraying! If the soil was sandy or organic, it wasn't to be used at all. A laconic footnote announced that it was 'harmful to fish'. I'll bet it was!

Some of the organo-phosphorous compounds carried a warning that stock must be kept away for between *4 and 6 weeks*, though nobody seemed to care how – or if – wildlife could be induced not to stray into danger. Metaldehyde, which killed my heron, was simply labelled 'Dangerous to game, wild birds and animals'. Such filth is still spilled wholesale on the land, and the slug pellets that contain it are more lethal than they would appear at first sight.

Herons do not eat slug pellets – and would be unlikely to eat slugs on open fields, though they probably eat any water-snails which catch their sharp eyes.

But frogs and toads eat snails and slugs – and herons eat frogs. Predators catch unhealthy prey more easily than active, healthy animals and weeding out the weaklings ensures the survival of the fittest to breed. So my heron probably died from eating a dying poisoned frog which had eaten a dying poisoned slug. That is how dangerous the foul stuff is and there can be no excuse for exposing wildlife to such risks to make a few agro-chemical fat cats fatter.

Rachel Carson's strictures were so powerful and so urgent that they caused enough public outcry to limit the use of some of the most dangerous poisons and to shame the Ministry of Agriculture to issue its explicit annual for a number of years.

Sadly, time has dulled the urgency of Rachel Carson's message, the Ministry of Agriculture's booklet was replaced with other milder and less explicit versions and the public heat died down. Precautions on the labels of products sold still preach the message to those who stop to read them – but the continued sale of a range of poisonous substances, many of them worse than slug pellets, is an indication of the continuing scale of the problem. An indication of the cynical irresponsibility of bureaucracy could not be given more clearly than in the case of the peanuts poisoned with aflatoxin.

Here was a natural mould infection so dangerous that people in America had died from eating peanut oil or butter. The fatal mould was produced by keeping peanuts – or similar substances – in hot and humid conditions.

The government, quite rightly, decreed that *all* imported peanuts should be tested and proved safe for people and domestic stock, so you and I are unlikely to die of aflatoxin poisoning.

The inexcusable irresponsibility lay in the fact that *rejected* peanuts (because they had been *proved* to be dangerous) were not destroyed. Our bloody enterprise society *allows* the rejects to be sold for wildbird food, because wildbirds don't matter unless they interfere with profit!

I discovered this servile grovelling to big business purely by accident. Otherwise I could have fed my badgers on nuts which the ministry were well aware were lethally contaminated and which they had cynically unloaded to the pet trade market because profit is paramount. The type of people who proclaim that it is all right to feed blue tits (which have no commercial value) on nuts which would poison 'domestic' cage birds are truly beneath contempt!

I have always reckoned that the basic stockmanship, which enables me to produce a surplus of pressured species, is precisely similar to the basic skills I use for the good of my table.

I have said that Jess and I have never bought an egg in more than 50 years of married life because we have kept our own free range hens under conditions which allow them to enjoy full and natural lives.

I have already mentioned that Jess and I rear free-range cockerels for the table. Every spring I buy twenty-four day-old cock chicks from a firm which produces birds for the 'chicken-in-the-basket' trade. These chickens are usually intensively reared so scientifically that they are as big as partridges, ready to kill, at eight to ten weeks old; I, however, rear mine under an infra-red light to keep them warm, instead of under a broody hen, and let them run, totally free-range, in a grassy paddock for the next five months. By November the survivors are huge, killing at 10–12 lb apiece, with the firm, succulent flesh of birds which have enjoyed an active, natural life till full maturity.

I state specifically that the *survivors* come to the table. Out of twenty-four day-old chicks I am very lucky to rear eighteen to maturity, because the clever scientists who bred them intended that they would be ready for market at ten weeks old: as they are programmed to die at ten weeks, their prospect of survival longer is of no account. But how do they get them big enough in such a short time? My birds would not be ready for customers to gorge on till long after ten weeks old.

My friend Michael Swales had been puzzled by the same conundrum, and had arranged for his senior students to conduct a sophisticated, controlled experiment in growth rates of poultry of differing types on differing diets. As part of this experiment he wished to examine the effects of the hormones used to promote growth in commercial 'broiler' flocks. The hormone additives he ordered were accompanied by detailed instructions which specified precautions to be taken in their handling. These included the use of protective clothing and avoidance of skin contact, inhalation, etc. Not wishing to be responsible for abnormalities among his students, he sent the additives back by return and ordered pre-treated, ready-to-feed diet.

The chickens grew so fast on this diet that their legs would not support their weight and by eight weeks old they literally staggered to the troughs, where they seemed to be hooked on the food which they gorged despite the discomfort it obviously caused. The whole experiment proved most unpleasant and nothing would have induced those who witnessed it to eat the flesh so obviously stuffed with unnatural growth promoters.

It really does seem that people prepared to grow rich by such unnatural treatment of intensively kept stock must be totally devoid of imagination or scruples or compassion.

Intensive husbandry of deer – which are not suited to such treatment – poses some possibly lethal threats to wild deer. The species is designed for browsing a mouthful here and there, often of leaves of trees and shrubs well above ground level. It is not designed for grazing ground herbage where other deer are excreting, with the result that resistance to disease transmitted by the urine and excrement of other deer is not good. Strength is lent to this theory by the abnormally high incidence of tuberculosis in intensively farmed deer, which sometimes approaches 30 per cent.

Some may say that this is a matter between the deer farmer and his deer and that, if he uses unnatural forms of husbandry, he must bear the loss. Human nature being what it is, deer farmers whinge for compensation for compulsory slaughter – whoever is to blame. The claims might be more numerous but the TB test for deer is far from satisfactory and the true percentage incidence may be higher than statistics show.

What is of greater concern to country lovers is that the practice of keeping deer under farm conditions may result in infected escapees passing TB on to wild deer, where it can be neither monitored nor controlled. Those of us who have been involved in trying to limit the extermination of badgers on the spurious evidence that they transmit bovine TB (which has never been proved) can imagine the public outcry there would be about efforts to annihilate whole deer populations, which had been infected through human greed.

I once hand-reared a white fallow fawn, which lived in our wildlife reserve for seventeen years, breeding fourteen fawns by wild bucks. She remained hand-tame, and very greedy, all her life and would gallop out of the wood when I rattled a bucket of corn. The other deer, which had never been handled, saw the old doe feeding and assumed that, if it was safe for her, it was safe for them. She acted as a decoy and objective observers could easily have been misled into assuming that, because they were so fearless, the deer in our reserve had, in effect, become domesticated. They would be wrong. When the old doe died the other deer in the wood, having no leader to act as decoy, reverted to the normal shy behaviour of the species. It would be as cruel to cram them into a cattle truck and drive them to a slaughter-house, stenching with blood and panic, as it would any other wild animal. Yet modern 'hygiene' requirements of the European Community press for farmed deer to be slaughtered along with other farm stock in conventional abattoirs.

We have to cull a percentage of our deer every year to keep the total herd number in balance with the available food supply. They die where they stand, from a single shot, by a skilled marksman with a high-powered rifle. They know nothing of their impending fate. All such slaughter is unpleasant but, when it is unavoidable, there is no excuse either for taking unnecessary risks of spreading disease by overstocking or unnatural husbandry, or for inflicting an undignified end in the name of intensive efficiency.

Field sports also have much to answer for though, properly conducted, shooting and conservation (of everything but game) need not be incompatible. Plenty of good sportsmen shoot pheasants and other game without exterminating every predator on suspicion that it has destroyed, or will destroy, all the pheasants before they can be shot. Some of the best naturalists I know are fond of the sport of shooting. The snag is that so much shooting today has fallen into the hands of rich syndicates who do not seem to understand the ethics of sport. With these people it is an exceptional day if no beater or shooter gets a peppering of shot, and one guest on a local shoot shot his host's yellow Labrador, believing it to be a fox!

Foxes, of course, are considered fair game by such gatherings, as are hawks, owls and other predators, whether legally protected or not. Badgers die, illegally but unmourned, if they stick their necks in snares set legally for foxes, and I have had periodic trouble with various local shooters, though I make it a rule to bait their birds into our wood – where they get a one-way ticket – if I have grounds to suspect that 'our' badgers are in peril if they stray over their boundary. A reputation for such hard-faced eccentricity limits the aggro when once it is understood that the word 'bluff' does not appear in one's vocabulary!

Nevertheless, a roll-call of potential opposition which still threatened to frustrate our ambitions to leave 'our' bit of Britain better than we found it was pretty daunting. When Big Brother gets his snout in the trough and his business cronies smell profit, the chances of forcing them to behave responsibly certainly seem slim.

NINE

IN TRUST

My strictures on those who defile the countryside may seem harsh because constructive alternatives entail painful compromise. Sensible give-and-take is vital to make room in the country for all who care about it.

The vested interests, which asset-strip our rural heritage, seem to have the balance of power tilted in their favour, for the chap on the train who forecast that I had no chance of beating such big money had used commonsense and precedent to calculate the odds.

I am happy to record, from my personal experience, that his prophecy that I was backing a loser has proved to be unfounded because stonecold certs do not always win.

A popular television series by a large – in every sense! – management consultant dispensed advice to 'old fashioned' companies on how to survive and prosper in our get-rich-quick society. His main secret of success seemed to lie in persuading clients to invest in hi-tech automation so that they could 'slim down' their labour force.

Similar clichés exuded from every sweating pore. It was the trendy jargon for making skilled craftsmen redundant and replacing them by fewer, cheaper, button-pushing zombies, who can punch-up escalating profits but are instantly dispensable if the balance sheet blips.

My ears pricked up when it was announced that Morgan Motors were to be one of the guru's guinea pigs because I was the proud owner of a succession of six Morgan sports cars after I graduated from racing motorbikes.

It was pure pleasure to watch Peter Morgan give the smooth would-be consultant his comeuppance.

When he churned out his patter about jettisoning skilled men, Morgan declined. He had no wish to join the gang who grow ever richer by mass producing infinite numbers of identical throw-away lookalikes. Quality counted with his customers and his workforce.

He explained, with dignity, that he already made enough money to meet his simple needs. Many of his employees – and their families before them – had been associated with the company since his own family founded it. He had no intention of prostituting his reputation by chucking skilled men and old friends on the scrapheap for profit.

It was precisely the medicine which could cure the rot which threatens the future of the countryside.

Fear of being victims of 'slimming down', for commercial reasons totally beyond their control, has spawned the insecurity which is filling every village with fugitives from the urban rat-race. Our own village has more than doubled in size in a couple of decades and a high proportion of the in-comers are a shifting population.

I started as the dog's body's dogsbody in the factory where I spent a third of my life, and I finished on the Board of Directors, not because of any great technical ability or family connections. I scrabbled to the top because I forged a bond of mutual trust with the workforce who pulled out all the stops to share success because they had implicit faith that I wouldn't slim them down just as we made the grade.

That couldn't happen now. Promotion does not come to those who work their way up from the shop floor. Young executives are expected to have gained 'breadth of experience' by working for rivals and – if possible – stealing the secrets of their trade. So young yuppies, who arrive in our village as a status symbol, rarely stay long. They soon move on to other villages, where they settle in more imposing houses, with flashier status symbol cars and even bigger mortgages. They ascend, in ever-decreasing circles of upward mobility, till they disappear, without trace, when somebody even brighter and more ruthless slims them down.

The inevitable result is that *anything* which purports to find employment is the flavour of the month. Speculative developers of the most hideous, cheap-jack housing 'estates' to defile the countryside have no difficulty about getting planning permission if they promise it will find jobs. What sort of jobs does not seem to matter. There may only be temporary, part-time work for a floating population of cut-price student labour but, if there are jobs of some sort, more red lights can flicker in corridors of power, at the local town hall, than down urban streets of easy virtue.

It would surely be more reasonable, if machines really are to be men's slaves instead of their masters, for Government to concentrate on ways of allowing us to benefit from the advances of technology to work less hours and have more time for leisure?

The materially successful among our grandparents had maid-servants to do the boring chores and gardeners and grooms to make certain that there was no irk in their masters' work.

Surely it would not be unreasonable, in our more civilized age, where manual chores have been eliminated by technology, that what work is left should be shared out over a shorter working week for all instead of full employment for some and slimming down for the unlucky ones?

Such simplistic solutions meet no approval from our permissive, multi-racial, multi-cultural enterprise society. Ever more 'liberal' laws allow a deluge of immigrants to flood in and compete for what work is available or be subsidised from your taxes and mine if they cannot, or will not, make the grade. After a couple of crippling world wars in my lifetime, we encourage those who lost them to invade our shores and win the peace.

Having worked closely with badgers for longer than I worked in industry, I have every respect for the way such problems are dealt with in nature.

Badgers are highly territorial and will not allow badgers outside their own social group to trespass into the habitat they need for food and residence.

The precise size of territory they defend may vary according to the current food supply but, if we substitute 'food', in badger society, for jobs, in ours, the problems are analagous. Badgers might teach bureaucrats a lot about priorities!

Not only do we allow strangers to compete for a declining number of jobs but medical science has lowered infant mortality and increased life expectancy.

Like it or not, the future will provide more time for leisure, whether enforced, because there are not enough jobs to go round, or because increased efficiency has reduced the hours it is necessary for us to work. Since the predictable trend will be for more and more urban dwellers to migrate to villages, competition to use every available rural yard for leisure is bound to escalate.

The wide-boys of our enterprise society have jumped on the wagon to create a leisure industry, and the Leisure Revolution it has spawned is already imposing intolerable pressures. The devil once found *work* for idle hands to do. Now he makes fortunes finding anything but work to fill in the hours of enforced inactivity.

One of the gravest problems in the countryside is that so many of the leisure pursuits competing for a foothold are totally incompatible.

Fishermen could enjoy their quiet, contemplative sport if speed-boaters did not insist on shattering the silence and stirring up the mud on the same lakes and reservoirs at the same time. Birdwatchers wish to observe the same birds the sportsmen come to shoot and walkers wallow knee-deep in mud where pony-trekkers trek or motor-cyclists scramble.

The most powerful modern Canute cannot halt the tide of change but it should not be beyond our wit to channel the flow of incompatible rural intrusions where they will cause minimal interference with the needs of others. All that is needed is civilized compromise.

Alton Towers, modelled on Yankee Disneyland and substantially funded with Yankee dollars, is often cited as the perfect model tourist attraction.

Back in 1980 there were a quarter of a million visitors a year. Now there are ten times as many! The doctor in the village was reputed to need a police escort if called to an emergency at weekends because traffic jams in local lanes make London commuter 'rush' hour seem like a racetrack.

Alton Towers was originally built as a country residence by the Earls of Shrewsbury. A standard history of Staffordshire describes Alton as 'having the magic of Prospero, with something of the cloud capped towers, the gorgeous palaces and solemn temples in its dreamlike setting'. It describes how John Talbot, the 15th Earl of Shrewsbury, spent the last 13 years of his life changing the surrounding 600 acres into an 'earthly paradise'. When he died, his nephew carried on his work, making it one of the most famous English country houses. The history concludes: 'Rarely has it been given to two men, the earls who began, continued and ended all this, to bequeath to posterity so fair a heritage of beauty and splendour.'

And what has become of that 'fair heritage' now? It is a bloody funfair!

Not only has the inspiration of the dedicated earls been obscenely debauched, but the lovely Churnet Valley, vitally important for wildlife and once a sanctuary of peace for stressed people to unwind, has also been choked by the sheer mass of casual gawpers.

Such totally incompatible intrusion into quiet and beautiful country is sheer sacrilege, in my eyes. I know how the locals must feel and the effect such pressure of visitors must have on wildlife because my own reserve and the adjacent re-creative conservation by the Forestry Commission in Bagot's Wood so nearly suffered a similar fate.

Surely visitors to such funfairs could as easily wet their knickers in fright on Big Dippers and Thunder Loopers and Hurdy-Gurdies in the middle of dense pine woods, where they would be a nuisance neither to man nor beast?

John Broome, who started the venture at Alton in a small way, with 250,000 visitors a year, is reputed to have flogged it for £60 million to finance an even better funfair on the site of Battersea Power Station.

Bully for him! A right and proper honeypot for visitors who may be lured away from sensitive, secluded countryside where too many people inflict intolerable pressure.

If the present proprietors of Alton Towers really had £60 *million* to spend, they could surely have spent a few of them in levelling some worked-out surface coal site or derelict industrial estate and throwing up a high enough mound to camouflage its vulgarity when it had been planted with trees.

I expect their answer to my impertinent suggestion would be that siting a mini-Disneyland in matchless country, like the Churnet Valley, would attract *profitable* tourists to the area. The fact that deflowering the charm and choking the access roads might kill the goose that laid such golden eggs does not occur to them.

It is inescapable that the flood of townsfolk back to the countryside will do irreparable damage if the market forces of our vaunted enterprise society are not disciplined. If the nettle is grasped and conflicting demands are sensibly zoned there will still be space and seclusion for generations as yet unborn.

Even the most peaceful pastimes need mutual goodwill to avoid friction.

Walking in beautiful country is among one of the most popular modern pastimes but visitors should remember that most footpaths were made by friends, for the convenience of friends to get to work or the village or school. They were never designed for leisure for the simple reason that folk then worked six days a week and went to church on Sunday. There was precious little time for leisure but rural populations were sparse and everyone knew his neighbours. It was common courtesy to allow them to cross one's land as a short cut and, if the route happened to pass close to the house, so much the better because local gossip was doubly welcome before daily newspapers grew fashionable.

Real countryfolk simply do not walk through growing crops. They would think that to do so was as bad mannered as walking over one's host's carpet in muddy boots. When crops were growing in a field the civilized thing to do was to walk round the edge.

Where paths originally passed through farmsteads or private gardens, it seems perfectly logical to agree to a diversion, so that the owner can still enjoy his privacy and unscrupulous visitors, wishing to 'case the joint', cannot use a legitimate right of way for a reconnaissance to avoid detection when they return to 'crack the crib'.

In my own village, there is a large girls' boarding school which has been extended over the years and has brought a great deal of trade and employment to the area. As it expanded, footpaths which presumably once went round it or were established for employees to get to work were included in the extended grounds, and it was not possible to prevent their use by anyone who wished.

The consequence was that an intruder, legally using the public footpaths, was able to break into the study bedroom of one of the girls, whom he raped. Despite this, there is still opposition to what seems a perfectly reasonable request for a diversion, though such obduracy seems to be totally irresponsible.

Sportsmen in the countryside also have much to answer for because what appears to be unreasonable behaviour of both sportsmen and their critics leads to unnecessary friction.

Hunting and shooting are perfectly legal, traditional rural pursuits and some of the most beautiful and typical English scenery owes its origin to country sports. A glance at an ordnance map will disclose an attractive random patchwork of little woods and spinneys and fields originally planted to encourage foxes and pheasants to provide sport for the owners of the great estates.

Sadly, the sportsmen who sired such scenery have been replaced by a new breed which contains a high proportion of urban get-rich-quickers who hunt, or shoot in syndicates, as a yuppy status symbol. They think that, because they've made a bit of brass, their wealth has brought not only the land they own but the rest of the countryside, which they gallop across with arrogant bad manners.

Few townsfolk, settling in the countryside, have any practical experience of country (or 'blood') sport. They fall easy prey to the anti-sport activists, who campaign ceaselessly to have *any* type of hunting with dogs (or hounds!) made illegal. Their strident message raises philosophical issues which are often out of context with reality.

I neither hunt nor shoot, for sport, myself, but I can see quite different ethical issues.

Some object to 'blood' sports because they believe they pander to primitive instincts and it is wrong that people should *enjoy* such pursuits. I regard it as no business of mine what other people do or do not enjoy and I regard passing judgement on them as pompous impertinence.

The other reason for objecting to hunting is that it is *cruel* to the quarry and this is a view with which I have sympathy. But, being a practical countryman, I am painfully aware of the results of alternative methods of 'controlling' foxes, which those who keep free-range hens, or sheep or pheasants, consider vermin to be caught by whatever means are available. Having seen foxes which have perished legally but slowly and painfully by strangulation in wire snares, I wonder. Having seen them creep away wounded to die of gunshot wounds or dying, illegally, from poison bait, I do not believe that sudden death when caught by a pack of hounds is any worse. None of the predictable causes of a fox's high risk ends is very pleasant.

What really infuriates me is the totally illogical sentiment which proclaims that it is all right to hunt some animals with hounds but not others, depending on whether the quarry is rated 'nice' or 'nasty'. Stags, in public imagination, are 'noble' and 'beautiful' and 'majestic' and must not, therefore, be hunted. Mink, which avoid ending as fur coats for glamour pussies may or may not be hunted, dependent on the political convictions of the activists. Rats are rated 'nasty, dirty' brutes and nothing is too bad for them.

The puddled oafs, who make such distinctions, fail to appreciate that rats feel exactly the same traumatic panic and stress and pain as deer or hares or foxes. What is sauce for venison should surely be sauce for the other items on the menu. Either all or none!

I find it rather sick that such subjective judgement should tear apart institutions as august as the Church and the National Trust.

There was great pressure on the Church to ban hunting on Church lands and the decision to look the other way was taken, not on objective judgement on the degree of cruelty, but because it was thought a ban might hurt the feelings of rural churchgoers, not the feelings of the quarry! Solomon, please note.

The National Trust paddled themselves up an even more un-navigable creek. They accepted millions of pounds' worth of gift property on the strict understanding that hunting should continue on land owned by the Trust unless it was made illegal.

But members of the Trust, who were anti-sport activists, narrowly passed a resolution demanding that all hunting with hounds should be banned on Trust property unless it was made illegal.

The Council was then faced with the decision whether to ignore the demands of members, constitutionally expressed, or whether to abide by solemn promises to owners, when they donated their estates, that hunting should continue in the future, as it had in the past, unless it was made illegal.

My own bitter criticism of the hunting fraternity is that they maintain it is their inalienable right to send a terrier to ground when hounds lose a fox that goes to earth.

I have spent so much time and effort trying to make it more difficult for badger baiters to obtain victims for their vile 'sport' that I would go to any lengths to oppose anyone who makes convicting badger diggers and baiters more difficult. The standard excuse, when caught using terriers to dig a badger out of his sett, is: 'We thought it was a fox' – for digging foxes is perfectly legal.

If it was made illegal to put any terrier to ground to dig out a fox or other quarry, anyone caught using a terrier could no longer claim that he thought it was a fox.

The fox-hunting lobby has so far proved too powerful politically to be forced to give up digging out their foxes. The only concession they need make to meet such a reasonable request would be to allow a fox that had beaten hounds and gone to earth to live to run another day.

The law would have been amended long ago if the hunting lobby had not got sporting (!) MPs to talk it out when they were unable to muster enough votes to defeat it by logic.

Such tactics bring no credit on either MPs or arrogant huntsmen and they will get no sympathy from me if public opinion grows incensed enough to have hunting made illegal.

Examples of powerful pressure groups imposing conditions which could alter or destroy rural ways of life – for better or worse – are very common.

Greedy agrochemical tycoons seduce farmers to spew more and more chemicals on the land to grow ever higher mountains of unsaleable crops.

There are those of us who think that it would be more environmentally responsible to give incentives *only* for wholesome quality instead of for vulgar quantity. This would reduce the surplus mountains of food and make healthy organic crops more economic to grow and buy.

It came as no surprise to me to get evidence that pressures and competition for the shrinking countryside are intense and still growing, and if the laws of the economic jungle are not tightened and enforced, the damage will be terminal. The size of organizations competing for influence over the quality of the environment is often reflected by the bureaucratic departments with similar objectives.

When the Forestry Commission refused to sell the lease on Bagot's Wood, so that the freehold could be sold for a holiday camp, I was very surprised by a leaked District Council Report demanding that the local MP should lead a delegation to the Minister of Agriculture to force the Government to overrule the Commission's refusal to sell the lease.

It seemed to be grossly impertinent for minor local officials to dictate to a government department how it managed land it held, more especially as the Commission claimed that land in its possession was, in effect, Crown property, which was immune from interference by minor local authorities.

The mystery was partially explained by another leaked letter. It was a personal letter to the District Head of Public Services from the Countryside Commission. It claimed that 'in 1985 the Commission sponsored the sale of Forestry Commission land at Pittance Park, in Nottinghamshire, to Center Parcs' – which, the writer claimed, 'was in the public interest'. The letter continued, 'The proposal by Center Parcs to establish a holiday village in East Staffordshire could contribute to our policies...', which explained the confidence of the local council that, with such big wheels rolling, the Commission would be a pushover.

The spontaneous intervention of impartial and distinguished politicians of all shades of opinion nipped the project in the bud, but it was more than a year before I had an opportunity to test the water at the top level of the Countryside Commission.

In autumn 1990, it was announced that the Commission was to inaugurate the first National New Forest since William the Conquerer's time and that it would include the area of Needwood Forest where my own reserve was situated. A friend in the media fixed an 'accidental' meeting with Sir Derek Barber, then Chairman of the Countryside Commission, and I mentioned that my reserve lay within the boundaries of 'his' new forest and that it was possible that my experience of managing wildlife on my nationally-known reserve might be of help to him.

Once more I discovered that, *if* one can make contact at the highest level, concern for the environment takes top priority. Sir Derek wrote to confirm our meeting, adding, 'I am indeed grateful for your interest, enthusiasm and offer of guidance in regard to the forest. We need all the help we can get from good people like yourself who have so much expert and local knowledge. I am arranging for you to be kept in touch as matters progress and look forward to having your direct advice.'

Patrick Cormack convened a meeting at my house a few weeks later, to discuss the future of my reserve, and it may be significant that the Commission representative was not the minor official who had encouraged the local council to tilt at a windmill in their efforts to bring the Forestry Commission to heel, but Bob Roberts, the Countryside Commission's Head of Land Use Branch. He was most helpful and constructive, proving yet again that, *if* one can make contact at the highest levels of government organizations, concern for the environment – and not exploitation of its precious resources – take top priority.

My contact with Sir Derek Barber also provided confirmation of the fact that life at the top, in almost any field, is fraught with insecurity. He said that his chairmanship of the Commission was drawing to its close and that there were moves afoot to combine the Countryside Commission with the Nature Conservancy Council – which he opposed. As with take-overs in commercial organizations, such major surgery is more often performed with daggers than scalpels.

By coincidence, I received within a few days the Nature Conservancy Council's Annual Report, covering the period April 1989 to March 1990, giving details of the Conservancy's activities over the year. It was written by Sir William Wilkinson, the Chairman, who was retiring after seven years, and those who care about the environment as deeply as I do will feel bitter and very sad about the contents.

Sir William Wilkinson pulled no punches. He began by saying that his review marked the end of an era, the era of the Nature Conservancy and the Nature Conservancy Council. 'During this time Great Britain was treated as the ecological continuum it is.... The present period,' he said, 'will finish in April 1991.'

Having recorded solid achievements which are taken for granted by committed environmentalists, he dropped his bombshell.

'On 11 July 1989, the Secretaries of State for the Environment and Scotland, Mr Ridley and Mr Rifkind, followed shortly by Mr Walker for Wales, *without any consultation and without attempting any proper costings, or drafting of proposed legislation, announced the dismemberment of the NCC into three separate country agencies. They ignored the fact that Britain is an ecological continuum, that the UK has international obligations under a number of Agreements and Conventions and that the requirements of nature conservation need the same informed, scientific assessment across all three countries.*

'*We were angered at not being consulted, particularly as we had prepared a proposal which would have devolved powers and responsibility for the Countries while at the same time maintaining a GB overview and coherence* (my italics).'

Shades of the traumas experienced by so many fleeing the urban rat race! Small wonder that bitterness bites so deep, feeding our resolve to salvage what we can.

In 1982 the NCC did a general survey to decide which SSSIs were to be re-scheduled and which de-scheduled, largely, it seemed, to limit claims from owners wishing to make some change of use which would involve compensation if their request was refused. They proposed to de-schedule the east side of my wood, where the Forestry Commission had planted pines, and retain, as an SSSI, the heronry, in Holly Covert, and the flower meadow, on Daffodil Lawn, though there was no question of a claim by me.

The snag, from my point-of-view, was that the theoretical protection given by SSSI status can be largely outweighed by the detailed clerical clearance needed for the multitude of unorthodox investigations into practical methods of wildlife management for which my reserve is nationally known. Filling in the forms which feed 'the System' is very time-consuming.

The nests in the heronry had increased from 18, when we came, to 70 when the junior NCC official called to decide what was and what was not of special interest to scientists and he rubbed me up the wrong way when he informed me that he could prosecute me if I continued my experiments without his permission. Being allergic to filling endless forms to fuel some futile 'system', I was pretty forthright, as I described in *My Wilderness in Bloom*, and things got somewhat out of perspective.

Once more it was demonstrated that, if such problems can be brought to the notice of senior officials of the highest rank, the protection of the environment takes precedence over personal or political problems.

Eddie Idle, then Assistant Director for England, and Audrey Lees, a member of the Nature Conservancy Council and Chairman of the NCC Committee for England, called on me personally.

They conceded that, since I am totally committed to conservation, there was no question of *any* harmful operation being done by me. We reached a constructive compromise and they de-scheduled the reserve to avoid mountainous paperwork and we parted with mutual respect for each other, if not for 'the System'.

The decision was subsequently justified, because, despite the loss of SSSI status, the successful breeding pairs of herons increased until, by 1990, there were 106, close to 2% of the national total.

Almost as exciting to me was that the experiment I had tried, by introducing three pigs to the enclosed area of Holly Covert, was also extremely successful. After years of bare wiry feg grass, left after the goats had bark-stripped growing hardwoods and nipped off all natural regeneration, the pigs' rooting left random patches of fertile soil in which young oaks and holly, bilberry and wood sage and briar now fill my eyes with pleasure and supply food and breeding habitat for wildlife. Although they obviously cause *no* damage to the herons above, the mere fact that they grow in an SSSI would have meant potential arguments without the help of Miss Lees and Mr Idle.

The last and – in some ways – the most important partner was the Forestry Commission. Jack Chard, who was conservationist in the best, most practical sense, enjoyed the well earned title Conservator when I first met him in the 1950s. We were both founder members of the Mammal Society and served our stint on the Council. We were founder members of the Deer Society and his protege, Gerald Springthorpe, was a personal friend before Jack and I met. Gerald eventually became Head Ranger and was internationally respected for his knowledge and love of fallow deer. No-one has done more for the 'image' of the Forestry Commission.

He trained Bill Grant, who made conservation in Grisedale Forest a byword, in the art of deer management.

Based at Cannock Chase himself, he gave it a reputation comparable to Grisedale for wildlife conservation and facilities for the public to enjoy the wildlife he attracted without disturbing it.

Bagot's Wood is included in the area of responsibility of Cannock

Forest and John Fletcher succeeded the conservator, who followed Jack Chard, with dedication and distinction. Fletcher came out of the same mould as Chard and both were light years ahead of their time in truly creative conservation.

Springthorpe persuaded John Fletcher to allow him to create a Conservation Zone across the drive from my reserve which, as a by-product, acted as a staging zone where surplus wildlife produced in my reserve could settle temporarily, and then disperse gradually and naturally where the public could enjoy them.

The work which John Fletcher organized was the *selective* thinning of softwoods to allow *natural* regeneration of the precious native mixed woodland that made Needwood Forest famous till the end of the war.

It was truly pioneering work which is rare in our stereotyped society and one of the objectives was to 'persuade' some of my herons to move back gradually into the oaks of Bagot's Wood, which supported a heronry of about 40 nests at the turn of the century.

Military Valley, about $\frac{3}{4}$ mile from my reserve, as the heron flies, was once the site of this ancient heronry.

It is therefore vital to create an undisturbed 'buffer zone' from woodland opposite my heronry to a frost pocket, where pines struggled to live, but where heather seems to thrive.

Until it was planted with pines, after the end of the war, it was a lovely heathy site where nightjars churred – and the hope is that, when the habitat is managed specifically to produce conditions they love, the nightjars will return, followed by the herons when pines have been selectively thinned to allow the indigenous oaks to grow strong enough to support their nests.

It came as a shock not only to me but to the Forestry Commission itself, when the speculative developers, Center Parcs, made their bid to force the Forestry Commission to disgorge the lease so that the landowner could cash in by selling the freehold for an astronomic sum.

When we arrived in 1963 there were no less than five oak trees marked as individual specimens on the Ordnance map in this area of Needwood Forest. It is superb natural oak country.

So John Fletcher put his whole reputation and career on the line by flatly refusing to sell the lease. He naturally obtained clearance from Forestry Commission Headquarters for this courageous stand and, when the Center Parcs speculative development was publicized, the Commission gave a formal 'No'! At that stage it was not known that the Countryside Commission was backing the local politicians so that the gravity of the threat was not appreciated. I entered the lists and gave it what publicity I could.

Out of the blue Norman Tebbit and no less than five politicians of cabinet rank wrote to support my stand, and I wrote to Raymond Johnstone, CBE, the Chairman of the Forestry Commission in Edinburgh, putting my case and asking for his help. He was particularly incensed to discover the little men on the district council were trying to outflank him by taking a deputation to the Ministry of Agriculture to force Government to overrule his decision. He told me that he was grateful for the information that the local council had got 'his' wood down on the structure plan as suitable for leisure development. With the advantage of hindsight, it seems more probable that the initiative came from some junior official of the Countryside Commission, who was thankfully overruled when I apprized Sir Derek Barber of the facts.

It also illustrates the ruthless pack law which destroys any civilized sense of security when different government departments are jockeying for the same prize.

The validity of the Forestry Commission's case depended on their hold of an impregnable 'buffer zone' between my reserve and their re-creative conservation zone $\frac{3}{4}$ mile to the west, in Military Valley.

John Fletcher regarded this as absolutely crucial to his case but, just at the critical time, he retired and was replaced by Roger Busby.

Nobody knew where he stood. Fletcher's reputation was built on deep and detailed knowledge about wildlife and its habitat. One of his predecessors had a name for caring for nothing but Commercial, with a capital 'C', forestry. My own impression, when I met him, was that he would not know the difference between a bull and a bulrush and might agree with the MP who said he thought newts turned into frogs.

Roger Busby had a reputation for sound commercial forestry but nobody seemed to know how far he would stick out his neck against potentially aggressive speculative developers or land-owners.

Raymond Johnstone, the Chairman of the Commission, wrote to tell me that he was not bound to let the shoot again after 1990/91 and before making a decision he would consider the sporting, recreational and amenity interests and would certainly take into account the points I made about the crucial importance of an adequate buffer zone.

Before the crunch came, Sir William Wilkinson, Chairman of the Nature Conservancy Council, had resigned and written his scathing, bitter criticism about the galaxy of government gaffes which had resulted in the emasculation of the NCC.

Sir Derek Barber, Chairman of the Countryside Commission, had also disclosed proposals to combine the Countryside Commission and Nature Conservancy Council, which would only perpetuate the shrill, eunuch chorus, easy prey for any manipulation and further exploitation, instead of protection of the environment.

Raymond Johnstone, still Chairman of the Forestry Commission, was the only survivor at the top of departments which had wielded influence when Center Parcs made the raid on Bagot's Wood.

Roger Busby, succeeding the redoubtable John Fletcher, was left to carry the can for decisions and policy entered into before he took responsibility for the conduct of silviculture in our neck of the woods.

It made me wonder if my tactics had been right. When the threat to the integrity of my reserve was at its height, I decided that I would write a book about it and publicize it as widely as possible in the media so that, if it did come to the crunch, the problem would be as familiar in government circles as Crichel Down. Hopefully the warning that the dereliction of the Industrial Revolution would be surpassed by the dereliction of the Leisure Revolution would sound enough popular alarm bells to ensure a Public Enquiry and the ensuing publicity would scupper the chances of incompatible development.

Speculative developers and the petty politicians they can sometimes manipulate have as many Achilles heels as a centipede and the media are always delighted to expose them if pointed in the right direction.

But with such in-fighting and scheming by government departments, pleas by individuals, however sound the arguments, will obviously lose their cutting edge if they don't conform with what would be regarded as more immediate priorities.

When even Prime Ministers can be knocked off the perch, sympathetic government ministers this week may be flogging sites for holiday camps next!

Even cabinet ministers, who may be world authorities on their own subject, are expected to abide by the convention that they do not use such specialist knowledge in constituencies other than their own without the consent of the sitting member. If, as sometimes happens, a local MP is in the pocket of local spec. developers, it is very difficult to get the best advice.

So I began to look round for other methods of making contact with the *current* specialist, of cabinet rank and the key, as always, seemed to be sheer vote-pulling potential.

To discover how much ordinary, uncommitted folk who make sacrifices to live in the country, really care, I wrote a deliberately provocative article with the cooperation of my friend, Simon Courtauld, who was editing a country magazine that enjoyed great respect and political clout while he was in the chair.

I deliberately trailed my coat and neither Simon nor I would have been surprised (or worried!) if I had been submerged by a torrent of abuse from outraged readers. We just wanted to test how strongly ordinary, uncommitted voters feel about protection or exploitation of the environment.

The title of the article was 'Codes of Conduct for Survival' and I began by examining natural ways of balancing supply and demand for basic resources. I pointed out that the greatest danger to the survival of a species – almost any successful species – is over-population. So, when the population of wildlife gets out of balance with the resources needed to sustain it, numbers are cut down by famine or disease. Myxomatosis in rabbits is a prime example which has been deliberately – some say wickedly – exploited by Man spreading the disease artificially to control the numbers of what he regards as a pest.

Over-population of people, in primitive communities, is also controlled by famine or disease but war has been used as well.

All wildlife has a strict code of species behaviour which is instinctively and rigidly followed. Recently, Man has been an exception. Medical research has increased life expectancy and lowered infant mortality.

Coincidental with this, there has been a catastrophic drop in the personal behaviour of our permissive society, which preaches that good manners are old hat and that previously rigid codes of conduct are now obsolete. It is no longer safe for young boys and nubile girls or old folk to wander alone in the countryside; schoolboys use knives instead of fists to settle disputes and even grandmothers are not safe from rape or mugging.

At the same time there has been a sharp decline in standards of behaviour, including the tolerance of unnatural practices in sexual behaviour. I was reared in a generation when sodomy was a crime and homosexuals were socially ostracized. 'Gay' was a respectable term for 'light-hearted, sportive, showy and brilliant', as my old dictionary still defines it.

Nowadays it is the polite term for buggery but those who complain about such practices are accused of eroding the civil liberties of our permissive society and being antisocial. The laws of Nature are not so easily bent because the consequence of such abberrations is the current invasion of Aids. It is a plague in every way as dangerous and certainly as fatal as myxomatosis but overpopulation is not necessary to spread it. It is the price of rejection of our immemorial sexual disciplines.

It was a deliberately provocative article, to test the climate of opinion on the defence of civilized behaviour, which includes maintaining the countryside inviolate.

We waited in vain for the anticipated torrents of abuse from trendy civil libbers. Letters deluged in all right, but they were friendly and incisive, almost all being supportive instead of vitriolic. The one exception came from a very cross psychologist, who said I had no compassion. I told him that he had confirmed my view that psychologists are often as batty as their clients and heard no more of him.

Far more important was the correspondence it generated from those who had saddled themselves with high mortgages and uncomfortable journeys to work through snarled-up rush hour traffic. They had made enormous sacrifices simply for the privilege of relaxing in peaceful places after the unnatural stress and insecurity of modern life.

There are hundreds of thousands of such refugees, flooding back on a tide as irresistible as the force which drove their ancestors from the countryside to towns. They care about the *unspoilt* quality of the countryside as deeply as any horny handed native, with whom they really have everything in common. I know because I have been on both sides of the urban and rural fences. They are as dedicated as I am to preventing the exploitation of pressured habitats, not just for themselves but for future generations. Such folk come from the most successful strata of society – or they couldn't compete for high-priced country houses. They are also exceptionally articulate – or they wouldn't be successful. And many of them work in the press or media, which gives them access to people of influence, including the most distinguished politicians, at whatever rhythm they are currently playing musical chairs to tip each other out of office.

Some measure of the potential influence such people can wield is the intensity of hatred they generate among the minor politicians and spec. developers, who plot fat profits by ripping off the countryside but are so often blocked by the adverse publicity generated by competently organized campaigns.

'*Nimbys*,' the minicrats spit, when their ploys for easy money and planners' gain are exposed. 'Not In My Back Yard,' is all they can reply to logical arguments for protecting sensitive, truly *unspoilt* areas.

It is the developers' parrot cry to denigrate any criticism of their plans to get rich quick and it aims to demonstrate that any impediment to enterprise development *can* only be selfish.

But the instinct for peace and tradition and wholesome values is far too deep to be gainsaid and, if the incomers to rural living can be combined, as a rural amenity lobby, with the existing powerful environmental lobby, it could be an invincible political force, to which socially responsible members of *all* shades would subscribe, whatever their party political differences, as I found for myself when men of cabinet rank, of both parties, came to the defence of the Forestry Commission, who were protecting my reserve. The developers may be able to tempt the minicrats, but the type of people I envisage to campaign against them have far more between their ears.

This might be less difficult to accomplish than it appears because Big Business, which is synonymous with entrepreneurs, is hypersensitive to public contempt and ridicule.

Michael Swales and I were recently walking round my reserve when I spotted an evil plastic balloon leering at me from a bramble brake.

I pulled it out and was furious to discover that it had been nibbled by a deer. I hoped it wouldn't die. Examination showed that it had emanated from Garfield Superloons. Garfield Superloos might have been more appropriate!

A day or so later, the local paper announced that forty *thousand* balloons were to be liberated, for charity, from Alton Towers. Since it was Keep-Britain-Tidy Year, there had been predictable complaints from environmentalists. So I phoned Alton Towers' press office and enquired if they had heeded the environmentalists' complaints. I was given a dusty negative answer.

I wrote my column, in their local paper, pointing out that, if I threw a balloon out of my car window or dropped one in the street, I would rightly be prosecuted as a litter lout. 'So why should Big Business be allowed to spew forty thousand over the countryside with impunity?'

The editor received a pained letter from the spokesperson, claiming that the balloons were certified '*Environmentally friendly and biodegradable*' but since environmentalists were unhappy, no more would be released. Perhaps unkindly, I did not let the spokesperson off the hook so easily. I wrote and offered to donate £10 to any charity he/she nominated, if he/she would allow the paper to photograph him/her eating one. My tenner is still in my pocket!

But the wooden spoon for prime bureaucratic inanity was reported under the heading 'Corpses in Copses'.

A northern city council, in a pathetic attempt to curry favour by proclaiming that its policies were 'Green', proposed introducing unmarked graves, in wooded glades, each with a tree planted over it, presumably to prevent escape or disturbance, till Judgement Day. This was designed to give the local minicrats a Green image, by enabling the dear departed to avoid disappearing in a puff of environmentally unfriendly pollution from the local crematorium.

Typical of his type, the little bureaucrat who dreamed up the scheme was so ignorant about what really goes on outside his city walls that it hadn't occurred to him that trees have only a finite life so that, when they decayed, there would be nothing to stop accidental disinterment by anyone who did not know there was a corpse in the copse. The hassles this would entail for the local constabulary, who would be called on to investigate whether death had been natural or from foul play, can only be imagined.

Whoever conceived such phoney public relations should have his ashes consigned to an egg timer, where he would do more useful work at no expense to the taxpayer.

The local ombudsman is kept in fulltime employment, in many areas, investigating complaints of unethical behaviour – or worse – by local politicians and bureaucrats.

Such publicity, if properly organized, can lead to police investigations, and *force* the zoning of incompatible development where it really does least damage.

The chap on the train and the man at the launch of the Institute of Environmental Assessment both told me that I was backing a loser if I pitted myself against such big money.

Now that the battle, if not the war, is won, they say that I could not have made my point if I did not have a high profile in the media.

My experience has convinced me that the combined voices of huge numbers of 'nimbys' would be far more effective but it is absolutely crucial that neither they nor the native countrymen, defending territory which belonged to their precedessors, should allow their opponents to drive a wedge between them and play off one faction against the other. As a combination they could be unbeatable in unison.

When Jess and I had notched up more than a century and a half between us, we searched around for some way to ensure continuity of management of our reserve when our heads had ceased to ache.

Patrick Cormack came up with the idea of forming a Trust and, after a great deal of discussion, we agreed the details.

Our decision was that a Trust should be formed to appoint and control a management committee, who are competent and willing to manage the reserve, in perpetuity, on the experimental lines I have described in *My Wilderness In Bloom*.

My friend Michael Swales, who has been interested in the work I have been doing here since before receiving the Countryside Award 1970, is retiring next year and is willing to be a trustee *and* supervise the management. As Chairman of the Staffordshire Wildlife Trust, he is ideally situated to continue and consolidate the partnership with the Forestry Commission, this time on an *official* basis! By guaranteeing a place on the management committee to the Staffordshire Wildlife Trust, expert help and advice could be made available to the Forestry Commission for the extension of their pioneering work in Bagot's Wood.

Gordon Beningfield, who had already consented to illustrate this book and write the foreword, kindly agreed to be one of the trustees.

Gordon and I have been close friends for years because we see eye to eye about the protection and management of our rural heritage and, apart from having a distinguished international reputation as a wildlife artist, Gordon is deeply respected as a champion of the environment by all who care about such matters. Jess or I or the subsequent owner of Goat Lodge will always be the other trustee.

Patrick Cormack will be Chairman of Trustees and he convened an exploratory meeting at my house, inviting the Chairman of the Forestry Commission, the Chairman of the Countryside Commission, the Chairman of the Nature Conservancy Council and the Chief County Planning Officer, to nominate senior officials of their departments, of decision making status, to attend the meeting. I invited Michael Swales and Roger Houghton, the publisher of this book.

As a result, Roger Busby, Forestry Commission Conservator, Bob Roberts, Head of Land Use Branch, Countryside Commission, and Dr Peter Knights, Regional Officer, Nature Conservancy Council, were nominated by the respective chairman of their departments. John Shryane, Chief County Planning Officer, came himself.

Jess and I had no means of knowing whether they would or would not be cooperative – so we didn't know whether to lace their coffee with rum or Exlax – but, as things turned out, everybody was most helpful and constructive. Not only did they promise the active help of their departments but they agreed to sit on an Advisory Committee, to meet at least once a year to monitor progress and help where possible.

The outcome of the discussion was that the conservator of the Forestry Commission undertook to maintain a secure buffer zone, undisturbed by shooting or other activities between my reserve and the Commission conservation zone.

Nobody could quarrel with this because the District Council and the landowner of the freehold of Bagot's Wood both stipulated that there would be such a zone when efforts were being made on behalf of Center Parcs to establish their holiday camp there. They actually offered a buffer zone of 200 acres in my unconditional sole ownership.

The landowner would obviously be pleased with the arrangement because he dislikes 'sterile softwoods', which the Commission is thinning selectively to restore naturally regenerated native hardwoods, for which Needwood Forest was so famous.

When the Commission has established its conservation zone, they have agreed to establish observation 'hides' on the western side of Military Valley, so that limited access, by permit, can be granted to members of the Staffordshire Wildlife Trust, under the supervision of Michael Swales. If a small charge is made for these permits, as by the Severn Trent Water Authority at Blithfield reservoir to members of the West Midland Bird Club, they would contribute to the administration costs, in line with the principles of my own reserve, which is self-financing. It would also be, to some extent, self-policing because paying permit holders, who regard their permits as a privilege because their numbers are limited to what the terrain can stand without stress, naturally take issue if others disturb it.

The buffer zone is such a closely wooded patch that it is difficult to flush birds over waiting guns so that a proportional reduction in rent would easily compensate for it being excluded, if the Commission decides to relet the shooting rights.

The remainder of Bagot's Wood, surrounding the farm in Bagot's Park, could be leased to the owner, at the Commission's discretion, thus fulfilling *all* the conditions stipulated by the Chairman in his communication to me. It could provide sporting rights where they are most useful, round the wooded periphery of the farm; there would be amenity and limited access on the western side of Military Valley conservation zone, where naturalists could enjoy the species conserved without disturbance.

The Nature Conservancy Council agreed to re-schedule the heronry, in Holly Covert, and the flower meadow, on Daffodil Lawn, to ensure continued protection when the ownership of Goat Lodge Reserve changes unpredictably, as is obviously likely with owners of the vintage of Jess and me. The fringe benefit of SSSI status would be added support for the Forestry Commission if development pressures were applied again.

This combination of sport, amenity and conservation also appealed to Bob Roberts, of the Countryside Commission, who proclaimed that 'the continued good management of the reserve is very important', and he promised assistance in making lasting provision for it, as did John Shryane, the Chief County Planner.

Dr Knights of the NCC stayed behind for a long discussion with Michael Swales and me and it was like the good old days of the Countryside Award 1970, re-establishing the same mutual trust and interest which was once taken as a matter of course. Dr Knights declared that the Nature Conservancy Council wished to take a positive part in ensuring that the reserve continue to prosper and he promised to send details for re-scheduling it as an SSSI to give support to the Forestry Commission's creative conservation project.

Patrick Cormack, as ever, demonstrated his own deep commitment to Heritage, in any form, by arranging for this book to be launched officially at the House of Commons.

It was indeed a memorable meeting, proving once more that socially responsible citizens, in every walk of life, share deep commitment to the long-term protection of the environment.

When Rachel Carson alerted us to the dangers of spewing poison on the land, the message was slow to take effect because smooth enterpreneurs played down the opposition as a bunch of selfish nimbys.

This time could be different. Growing numbers of highly skilled professional people are settling in the countryside precisely *because* they are dedicated to retaining the quality our forefathers took for granted and which we so nearly lost.

The object of their concern is precisely the same as that of those born and bred in the same parish and, with sensible mutual compromise, they will speak together with the voice of reason.

I have sometimes thought that mine is a very small and insignificant voice, crying in the wilderness, but when Jess and I decided to form a Trust to ensure the continuation of management of our reserve, it was immensely satisfying to discover that, far from being alone, we are part of the swelling chorus of those who have faith in the future.

So we arranged for the Trust to start while we are still around to share the work and pleasure. The Trust will start on the day this book is published.

INDEX